Sky Kings

Sky Kings

BLACK PIONEERS OF PROFESSIONAL BASKETBALL

by

Bijan C. Bayne

African-American Experience

FRANKLIN WATTS

A Division of Grolier Publishing
New York • London • Hong Kong • Sydney
Danbury, Connecticut

Interior Design, by Claire Fontaine

Photographs ©: AP/Wide World Photos: 23, 39, 67, 69, 84, 92, 94, 116, 124; Basketball Hall of Fame: 30, 52, 58, 110; Booker Brown: 25; Miles Educational Film Productions, Inc.: 20; Transcendental Graphics: 45, 51, 89; UPI/Corbis-Bettmann: 14, 37, 41, 63, 101; UPI/Corbis-Bettmann: 122.

Library of Congress Cataloging-in-Publication Data

Bayne, Bijan C.
Sky Kings: Black pioneers of professional basketball / Bijan C. Bayne.
    p. cm — (African-American experience)
    Includes bibliographical references and index.
Summary: Describes the history of African Americans in professional basketball, from the
    traveling teams in the first half of the century to the stars of the 1960s.
    ISBN 0-531-11308-6 (lib bdg.)   0-531-15900-0 (pbk.)
1. Afro-American basketball players — Biography. 2. Afro-American basketball players — History.
[1. Basketball — History. 2. Afro-Americans — Biography.] I. Title II. Series
    GV884.A1B39 1997
    796.323'092'2 — dc20

[B]   96-38708
                                            CIP
                                            AC

Contents

Sky Kings

Introduction

The contemporary image of a professional basketball player is that of a black male. That image is personified by the smiling faces of Michael Jordan, Shaquille O'Neal, and Grant Hill, who endorse various products before a national television audience. For 20 years, two-thirds of the players in the National Basketball Association (NBA) have been black. Pro basketball was the last of the three major U.S. sports to integrate its major league, but it was years ahead of football and baseball in hiring a black head coach and in featuring an all-black major sports team. (The Boston Celtics led the way, achieving both milestones in the middle 1960s.) Although the presence of black basketball players in the NBA is taken for granted today, two generations ago black men and women who were paid to play the game were confined to joining all-black touring teams that traveled the country cheaply in buses and cars. Often these early professional teams played in dance halls or

YMCA gymnasiums. Their coach or business manager drove them to hastily scheduled games. The players had no insurance, no sneaker contracts, no agents, and no endorsements, and only a few black-owned newspapers covered their games. In the late 1930s, these players were signed for $125 a month.

There are many theories about why blacks began to outnumber whites in pro basketball in the late 1960s. Black Americans had become the predominant ethnic group in America's northern and eastern cities, replacing Irish, Italian, and Jewish Americans. Basketball is an affordable game for poor, urban children: The only equipment required is a ball and a hoop, which could be fashioned out of a milk crate or bicycle rim. Unlike baseball or football, basketball could be practiced alone. Before 1950, Jewish-American athletes dominated urban basketball and the New York City college game. As the populations in sections of Philadelphia and New York became more black than Jewish or Italian, black teenagers took up basketball, joining in the pickup games popular in school yards. Still, by the time the NBA signed its first black players in 1950, pro basketball was a minor sport in the United States. Teams struggled to fill arenas and switched cities frequently. More young blacks looked up to major-league baseball's few black players, the majority of whom played in New York.

The NBA's 50th Anniversary

To commemorate the NBA's 50th Anniversary, a committee of 50 NBA sportswriters, former stars, current and former coaches, and league officials selected the 50 greatest NBA players of all time. Their selections were announced on October 30, 1996. Six players featured in Sky Kings appeared on the list: Elgin Baylor, Wilt Chamberlain, Hal Greer, Sam Jones, Oscar Robertson, and Bill Russell. (Baylor, Chamberlain, Russell, and Robertson served as panelists.)

Today, basketball is clearly the most popular sport among America's youth. NBA teams and players generate more money from posters, team jackets, caps, trading cards, and other paraphernalia than professional football or major-league baseball teams do. More youngsters can identify with David Robinson and Kobe Bryant than with the top two or three baseball or football stars. The NBA has reached young people through telecasts of games, a stay-in-school program, and sales of athletic gear. This book tells the story of those blacks who paved the way for today's multimillion-dollar contracts and personalized shoes—the black pioneers of professional basketball.

CHAPTER 1

From Peach Baskets to Ballrooms

In 1890, a Canadian named James Naismith enrolled at the Young Men's Christian Association (YMCA) school in Springfield, Massachusetts. The school trained athletic directors and YMCA secretaries. Naismith had studied for the ministry at McGill University, a prestigious Montreal college. He eventually accepted a teaching job at the Springfield YMCA and was charged with developing an athletic activity to occupy young men between football and baseball season. The activity would have to be one that could be played indoors during the cold Massachusetts winter.

No one is sure where Naismith got the inspiration for the new sport that he developed. Some historians think he was invited to the YMCA in nearby Holyoke, Massachusetts, to observe a new game his associate, Dr. George Gabler, was trying out. Under Gabler's direction, YMCA instructor William Morgan had invented volleyball.

Naismith thought of the other sports then popular—football, water polo, field hockey, rugby, and soccer. An indoor team sport he envisioned would require a large, light ball that would be easy to see and propel. The ball could be put in play at a center area of the playing space, as in rugby and water polo. Instead of putting the goals at floor level on each end, Naismith decided to elevate them. He asked his custodian to provide boxes to serve as experimental goals. The custodian could not find any boxes of the appropriate size, so he suggested using peach baskets. When the two baskets were attached to the running-track balcony that encircled the gym about ten feet above the floor, the game of basketball was born. Naismith devised the original 13 rules, which, among other regulations, required that the goals be elevated and prohibited players from running with the ball or making personal contact with each other.

This early version of Naismith's game, which spread primarily through YMCAs and tours in the Northeast, was very different from the sport played all over the world today. After each basket was made, a jump ball took place at center court. (This rule was not changed until the 1930s.) The earliest players did not dribble, or bounce, the basketball to advance it, but they were allowed to pivot without traveling violations being called. The first backboards were screens, and games were played in caged gymnasiums to protect fans—and to protect the athletes from unruly spectators. (That's how basketball players became known as cagers.) By and large most of Naismith's original 13 rules remain, including the five seconds allowed to the offensive team has to put the ball in bounds and the prohibition against the defense interfering with a ball in contact with the goal (goaltending). Shot clocks and lane rules came years later, as officials noticed aspects of the game that slowed play or encouraged roughhouse activity. The first basketball players wore long gray pants and knee pads and sometimes played with soccer balls.

Basketball became so popular that colleges were playing competitively by 1893. Other gym activities were no longer scheduled at

Dr. James Naismith holds a basket and a ball. Naismith invented the game of basketball at the Springfield, Massachusetts, YMCA in 1891.

YMCAs. The Philadelphia YMCA later banned basketball because people who wanted to play other games could never reserve gym time. Basketball teams in Philadelphia resorted to playing in warehouses or rented dance halls. Some games were nine-on-nine, depending on court size. Naismith's alternative winter sport had caught on fast.

Early Professional Teams

At the 1904 World's Fair in St. Louis, a basketball tournament was held on an outdoor grass court. Five teams participated, and the Buffalo Germans, a YMCA team, emerged victorious. Unlike today, at the beginning of the twentieth century YMCA teams, men's clubs, collegiate squads, and professional teams played each other. Intercollegiate play did not become separate until colleges formed athletic conferences, which were primarily organized for football. This period in basketball history saw two significant developments for blacks. The first recorded instance of a black American playing professional basketball was 1904, when Bucky Lew played with Newbury-Haverhill (Massachusetts) in the New England League. Three years later, Frank Wilson played with Fort Plain (New York) in the Mohawk Valley League. These loosely organized minor leagues provided a way for working men to make a few extra dollars during the winter.

In 1905, a black Harvard graduate, Dr. Edwin B. Henderson, founded the High School Athletic Association to encourage black interscholastic athletics. A year later, Henderson became physical education supervisor for black schools in Washington, D.C., where education and other aspects of public life were segregated at that time. Henderson organized the Interscholastic Athletic Association for the mid-Atlantic states, and under his direction track, football, baseball, and basketball programs improved measurably in black high schools in Washington, D.C.; Baltimore, Maryland; Wilmington, Delaware; and Indianapolis, Indiana. In gyms, churches, school yards, and alleys, black youngsters took to the fast-paced new game. In 1907, baseball was the only sport with a major professional league. Black Americans who played baseball, football, and basketball generally did so against other black players. Very few Americans of the early twentieth century earned money by playing sports—and only a handful of blacks did.

The Buffalo Germans were the first dominant touring professional basketball squad. Their style of play led to widespread use of the pivot and set screens. Another upstate New York team, the Troy Trojans, were so good that the leagues they played in, the Hudson River League and the New York State League, dissolved around them because of the Trojan's superiority. Troy won 38 consecutive games in 1914–15. Players wore cleats and played on 40 by 60 foot courts.

By 1925, the American Professional Basketball League (ABL) was well established under National Football League president Joseph F. Carr. Key owners of the ABL were laundry tycoon and Washington Redskins owner George Preston Marshall, Chicago Bears founder George Halas, and Cleveland department store mogul Max Rosenblum. Ten thousand fans had attended one 1924 Cleveland Rosenblums game. Many top ABL players were Jewish. None were black. The ABL played by Amateur Athletic Union (AAU) rules, which prohibited the two-handed dribble and mandated disqualification of a player after five personal fouls. The ABL boasted nine teams stretching from Boston to Chicago.

Another league, the Metropolitan League, survived from 1922 to 1928. From 1926 to 1928, the Original Celtics, based in New York City and owned by Jim Furey, were the champions of pro basketball. The Celtics starred Henry "Dutch" Dehnert, Nat Holman, Ernie Reich, 6'5" Joe Lapchick, and 6'4" Horse Haggerty. Touring the country in a luxury seven-passenger Pierce-Arrow automobile, they earned as much as $125 a game. Horse Haggerty eventually made $10,000 a season playing for the Original Celtics—an astronomical figure for those days.

16

The Renaissance Teams

While the all-white pro leagues were gaining in popularity, black basketball was making advances. In 1922, William Roche, an emigré from the Caribbean island of Montserrat, promoted movies and ballroom dances in the Renaissance Casino. The Renaissance was located at 135th Street and Seventh Avenue in Harlem, the famed black neighborhood in the upper Manhattan section of New York City. Robert Douglas, a Caribbean immigrant from the island of Saint Kitt's, saw his first basketball game in New York City in 1903. Douglas worked as a hotel doorman at 312 Manhattan Street near 114th Street. Together with two other West Indians, George Abbott and J. Foster Phillips, Douglas organized the Spartans Field Club, an athletic club for Caribbean immigrants who wanted to play cricket, soccer, track, and basketball. Douglas intended to name his newly formed basketball team the Spartans, after the amateur club.

Douglas asked William Roche whether he would book basketball games at the Renaissance. Roche didn't like the idea because basketball was a very physical game that drew rough crowds. He didn't want to lose his regular customers, so he refused the offer. Douglas told Roche that he would name the basketball team after the ballroom, bringing publicity to the dance hall. He also offered Roche a percentage of the gate receipts. Roche agreed to the deal.

In the team's first game, the Renaissance Casino team—nicknamed the Rens—beat the Collegiate Big Five 28-22. The first group of players at the ballroom games included Hy Monte, Frank Forbes, Leon Mande, and a professional baseball player, Clarence "Fats" Jenkins. (Forbes later became business manager for the New York Cubans, a baseball team in the Negro Leagues, and he was the first black judge on the New York State Boxing Commission. When Willie Mays joined the New York Giants baseball team in 1957 and moved to Harlem, Forbes was his mentor.)

The second Renaissance club featured George Fiall, James

"Pappy" Ricks, and Clix Garcia. The original team captain, Hilton Slocum, retained his position. Frank Forbes, George Anderson, Hy Monte, Leon Mande, and Harold Jenkins left the team, and in 1925, Clix Garcia was replaced by Harold Sanders. Eyre "Bruiser" Saitch was the only new player to join the team between 1925 and 1930. Saitch had been a standout athlete at New York's DeWitt Clinton High School and was one of the nation's best tennis players. He had won the American Tennis Association (ATA) men's singles championship in 1926 and been part of the ATA men's doubles championship team in 1928. (The ATA was an all-black tennis association; the United States Lawn Tennis Association did not admit blacks as members.) The Rens' female fans thought Saitch was the most handsome member of the team.

In 1932, Johnny Casey Holt replaced Harold Mayers. During a basketball contest prior to a Rens game in Cleveland, Robert Douglas noticed a tall, muscular young man who scored baskets with ease. The player was "Wee" Willie Smith, and the Rens signed him. At 6'5" Smith became the squad's tallest player, joining the club when Hilton Slocum retired after nine years as captain. The Rens drew the largest basketball audiences in the country. They attracted 11,000 and 15,000 fans on successive nights in Cleveland. Fifteen thousand turned out to see them in Kansas City, where the Rens visited nightclubs after their games to hear a new style of music called jazz.

Back-to-back games with the Original Celtics drew a combined 25,000 spectators. The Celtics, starring Joe Lapchick and Dutch Dehnert, figured prominently in the history of the Renaissance Casino team. With the 6'5" Lapchick, the Celtics were America's other superior touring basketball squad. One Celtics player, 6'4" Horse Haggerty, earned $10,000 a year, an impressive salary during the Great Depression. The Celtics set a record by winning 44 games in a row. The 1933–34 Rens doubled that, with 88 straight victories. The streak ended with a loss to the Celtics. (By comparison, the most consecutive wins in NBA history is 33 by the 1972 Los Angeles Lakers, led by Wilt Chamberlain. Before the Lakers' streak, the longest victory string was only 19.) That Rens squad—starring Saitch, Ricks, Jenkins, Smith, and Bill Yancey—is considered the strongest team the club ever assembled. They won seven of eight meetings with the Celtics.

Pappy Ricks left the squad in 1935. Jackie Bethards stepped down and was succeeded by Johnny Isaacs. Robert Douglas held annual tryouts for the Renaissance, which attracted two dozen hopefuls a year. He generously paid room and travel expenses for every young man who came to the tryouts. When Bill Yancey resigned from the 1936 team, Al Johnson took his place. (Yancey also starred for the New York Black Yankees of the Negro National League, and he became a major league baseball scout after the integration of baseball.)

The Renaissance team was paid monthly. Douglas bought them team buses, which he refinished and customized for their long road trips. Eric Illidge, a former college athlete, was the team's first coach. The Renaissance played some of their games in the Metropolitan Basketball Association, which included black and white teams. Known by the nicknames the Renaissance Big 5, Douglas's team was one of the most successful basketball teams in history. With such players as Wee Willie Smith, Johnny "Speed" Isaacs, Bruiser Saitch, and Casey Holt, they played nearly every day and twice a day on weekends. Sometimes they went months without losing. Some of America's best athletes played for the Rens. Three players—Fats Jenkins, Bill Yancey, and Zack Clayton—also played baseball in the Negro leagues.

By 1939, Al Johnson, Lou Badger, and Johnny Holt were gone, and new players included Pop Gates, a New York schoolboy legend from Ben Franklin High School and Clark College (Atlanta), and Clarence "Puggy" Bell, the most talented player from the Harlem YMCA. Together with defensive specialist Zack Clayton from Philadelphia's Central High School (which two decades later produced a basketball player named Bill Cosby), this team captured a world championship for the Renaissance. Fats Jenkins was the best

The Harlem Renaissance won the 1938–39 world championship of professional basketball. Pictured here are (left to right): Willie Smith, Charles Cooper, John Isaacs, William Gates, Clarence Bell, Eyre Saitch, Zack Clayton, and Clarence Jenkins.

known player on this version of the Rens. A former star at New York's Commerce High School, Jenkins was the team's captain and floor leader, and he played longer than any team member. Another longtime mainstay was Charles "Tarzan" Cooper, the burly pivot man who had come aboard in 1930. Cooper, Gates, and Clayton went on to play for the Harlem Globetrotters. (Clayton later refereed the 1974 Muhammad Ali–George Foreman heavyweight championship bout.)

In March 1939, the Chicago *Herald American* newspaper held a world tournament for professional basketball teams in the 20,000-seat

Chicago Stadium. The Rens beat the New York Yanks 30–21 in the second round and then defeated the upstart National Basketball League (NBL) champions, the Oshkosh All-Stars, 34–25 in the finals. In their 26-year existence, the Rens won 2,318 games against 381 losses. The team's second world championship came not as the Rens but after they were reorganized as the 1943 Washington Bears and led by standout Dolly King.

In a typical barnstorming campaign, the Rens traveled 38,000 miles in a year, and they played 140 to 150 games a year. Sometimes they played twice on Saturdays, three times on Sundays. They played as far west as Wyoming and as far south as Louisiana. In towns were there was no lodging for blacks, they slept on the bus. They carried food on road trips because most white-owned restaurants would not serve them.

At the team's peak in the 1930s, the Rens employed eight players; the highest-paid player, Pop Gates, made $1,000 a month. Players received three dollars a day in meal money. Prospective players from college and club teams made two or three dollars a day to scrimmage against the Renaissance squad. Doc Bryant was the team trainer, and Frank Richards the publicist. The team had a very good marketing strategy; their publicity office estimated that it distributed 200,000 posters a year.

In 1963, the Harlem Renaissance team was inducted into the Basketball Hall of Fame in Springfield, Massachusetts. Robert J. Douglas, the Rens founder, was named to Hall of Fame in 1971. He died on July 16, 1979.

Basketball's Spreading Popularity

Black newspapers chronicled the Rens' success, which helped popularize basketball among black Americans. America's second black basketball dynasty was based in Chicago. Dick Hudson, a former Chicago Bears football player, organized a team to play at Chicago's

Savoy Ballroom. Like the Rens, this team took the name of its dance hall. The nucleus of the Savoy Big Five was from the Wendell Phillips High School team, which in 1928 became the first black school to win a Chicago city championship. Savoy became as powerful in midwestern basketball as the Renaissance was in the East.

In predominantly white states, such as Minnesota and Wisconsin, few promoters would schedule the Savoy Big Five. Dick Hudson agreed to pay a cash booking fee to a 26-year-old promoter for every game that he could get for Savoy. The young promoter, Abe Saperstein, was a 5'3" former lightweight basketball player (high school teams in some regions were classified by weight). Paid by Hudson in advance, Saperstein found halls that would book the Savoy Big Five. Soon the team was earning $75 a game, divided into $10 shares for each player, $20 for Saperstein, and $5 for expenses.

Saperstein knew Chicago schoolboy basketball inside out. He hired the best players from the Wendell Phillips heavyweight teams for Savoy. In the late 1920s and early 1930s, there were not many college opportunities for black high school basketball players. Black colleges could not afford to offer athletic scholarships, and only a few major colleges recruited black athletes. Touring teams, such as Savoy and Renaissance, provided an economic chance for the few elite players of color.

Saperstein often booked the Savoy Big Five at Chicago's Eighth Regimental Armory. At first they played black college teams, such as

Reversing the Ban

In 1948, colleges in the National Intercollegiate Tournament in Kansas City signed an agreement barring black players from the championship tournament. Although it had no black players, Manhattan College declined its invitation to the prestigious tournament. Long Island University and Siena also withdrew from the invitationals. Tournament officials reconsidered their action and removed the ban on black players.

Abe Saperstein, photographed here in 1950, was the owner and coach of the Harlem Globetrotters.

Clark, Wilberforce, and Morgan State. Eventually Saperstein bought the team from Dick Hudson and decided it needed a more glamorous name. At the time Harlem was the cultural capital of black America. During the late 1920s and early 1930s period known as the Harlem Renaissance, such authors as Countee Cullen, Langston Hughes, Dorothy West, and Zora Neale Hurston, scholar Alain Locke, and painter Lois Malov Jones helped put Harlem on the map of world arts. Saperstein renamed the Savoys the Harlem Globetrotters. Until the NBA achieved worldwide popularity in the 1980s, the Globetrotters were basketball's most famous team.

The early black basketball teams played by legitimate rules. They did not play clown basketball (which the Globetrotters eventually became known for) featuring crowd-pleasing tricks against stooge teams.

Women's Teams

In addition to the Globetrotters, another Chicago team became a powerhouse in the 1930s. Ed "Sol" Butler, who had been a basketball star at Duquesne University in 1910, coached the Chicago Romas, a team of black women. The Romas starred Isadore Channels, Mignon Burns, Virginia Wills, and Corrine Robinson. They took on all comers and defeated most. Channels was also a great tennis player, winning four national singles championships in the American Tennis Association. Ora Washington, the greatest female player in ATA history, won 8 ATA singles championships and 12 straight women's doubles titles, but she was barred from entering white tennis tournaments. Washington also played center for a women's basketball team, the Germantown Hornets. She then joined the Philadelphia Tribune, a squad named for Philadelphia's leading black-owned newspaper. Under the women's rules of the day, the Tribune played six to a team: three women on offense and three confined to defense. Five-player, no-platoon basketball was considered too strenuous for young ladies.

In the 1930s, the Philadelphia Tribune team was a powerhouse in women's basketball in the east. They conducted clinics that introduced basketball to young black girls in the south.

With Ora Washington, Rose Wilson, Gladys Walker, and Virginia Woods, the Tribune won several eastern championships in the 1930s. In 1938 they conducted basketball clinics during their southern tour. These clinics helped spread basketball awareness among young black girls in the racially segregated South. In the wake of the Tribune's success, such athletes as Alice Coachman, Althea Gibson, Willie White,

Wilma Rudolph, and Jackie Joyner-Kersee went from high school basketball stardom to success in other sports.

Washington, D.C., had two strong women's basketball teams for black players, the Carlyles and the Deers. Like the Philadelphia Tribune and the Chicago Romas, these teams won the majority of their games. Blanche Comfort Winston, one of the elite athletes of her day, played for both the Carlyles and the Deers and was a tennis star as well. She won an ATA singles title in 1937. Before that, she had been a mixed doubles national champ in 1927 and 1928 and women's doubles champ in 1930 and 1931 with Ora Washington. Winston later managed New York's Saint Nicholas Basketball Club, and as an over-50 player she won the New York Tennis Association veteran singles championship.

The Rise of the Professional Leagues

During the Great Depression, an economic crisis that began in 1929, few American Basketball League games drew more than 2,000 fans. The Cleveland Rosenblums had the best attendance; on good nights they filled the 3,345-seat Cleveland Public Auditorium. Other teams in the ABL included the Brooklyn Visitations, the Paterson (N.J.) Crescent, and the Toledo Red Men. In 1933, basketball was largely an eastern sport. John O'Brien reorganized the ABL with a group of eastern teams for the 1933 season. One of the best teams was the Philadelphia Sphas, who originated at the South Philadelphia Hebrew Association. In 1936 the Sphas changed their name to the Philadelphia Hebrews. The ABL also featured the New York Jewels, a team centered around a superb college team nicknamed the St. John's Wonder Five. The Jersey Reds and the Wilmington Blue Bombers were also ABL members. (The Blue Bombers were still active in the Eastern Basketball League during the 1960s.)

A rival league, the Midwest Basketball Conference (MBC), began play in 1935. Economic depression in the United States was beginning to ease, and spectator sports were a popular outlet for the American working class. Babe Ruth and Ty Cobb had made baseball the national pastime, and football—with such stars as Red Grange, Bronko Nagurski, and Sammy Baugh—was next in popularity. Basketball was only popular in certain regions: urban areas in the East and large midwestern cities.

The MBC was made up mostly of teams sponsored by businesses: the Akron Goodyears, Indianapolis Kautskys, Fort Wayne (Indiana) G.E.s, and the Chicago Duffy Florals. Other MBC teams were the Pittsburgh Young Men's Hebrew Association and the Buffalo Bison, which had a black player, the 6'4" Hank Williams. Chicago won the first league title.

The National Basketball League (NBL), founded in 1937, was considered basketball's major league in the late 1930s. The league grew to 18 teams, divided into East and West divisions. The teams played a 28-game regular schedule, and teams scheduled extra games as they traveled, which was called barnstorming. One team owner, Gerry Archibald Warren, was the son of one of the original 18 men who played under James Naismith in the Springfield YMCA in 1891.

In 1941, Sheybogan (Wisconsin) and Toledo represented the NBL in the World Tournament at Chicago Stadium. Later that year, the United States was drawn into World War II by the surprise Japanese bombing of the U.S. naval fleet at Pearl Harbor, Hawaii. The devastating loss of American battleships and servicemen shocked the nation. Men of all ages and races volunteered for military service, even though some were unqualified because of age or physical limitations. Enlistment affected professional and college sports. Famous athletes became soldiers, sailors, or airmen, and women joined all-female corps.

Perhaps because of the shortage of capable men of any color, Toledo owner Sid Goldberg integrated his NBL team with four black players: Al Price, Casey Jones, Shannie Barrett, and Zano West. The Toledo squad faced problems on the road. Hotels would not house the team, and restaurants and diners refused them service. The 1942 Chicago Studebakers ran into the same obstacles. Named for an auto manufacturer, the Studebakers had two black players, Sonny Boswell and Rosie Hudson. (Boswell had a long career as a Harlem Globetrotter after his stint in the NBL.) The players worked in the Studebaker auto plant during the day. As veterans returned from the war, NBL teams released their black players.

The last league to challenge the NBL was the Basketball Association of America (BAA), which included the Chicago Stags, Providence Steamrollers, Philadelphia Warriors, and Boston Celtics. Its team owners were men with little or no prior basketball experience, although two BAA owners, Maurice Podoloff and Eddie Gottlieb, later became influential in the future of professional basketball. Most BAA players were military veterans, castoffs from other pro leagues, or former college stars. In 1946, college basketball was more popular than the pro game, but college basketball was rocked by a scandal in which players had been found to have fixed the outcome of games for gamblers by purposely not scoring, or shaving points. Fans grew to distrust the results of college basketball games, especially important games in New York's Madison Square Garden.

Major League Baseball and Pro Football Integrate

Race relations in professional football and baseball experienced a breakthrough in 1946. The Brooklyn Dodgers assigned Jackie Robinson, a former UCLA basketball star, to their Montreal farm team. They hoped that he would soon become the first black big-league baseball player. The Dodgers had scouted Robinson, who was playing for the Kansas City Monarchs of the Negro American League. Another UCLA athlete, running back Kenny Washington, was signed by the National Football League's Los Angeles Rams that same year. In 1947, both the Dodgers and Rams signed a few black teammates to play with Robinson and Washington, respectively. These first black pro athletes were made to feel unwelcome by many white teammates, taunted and physically attacked by opponents, and verbally abused by fans. When their teams traveled, the black men stayed in separate hotels from the other players. Black heroism in World War II apparently had not convinced many Americans that blacks were equal.

Many coaches thought black athletes were not decisive, intelligent, or courageous enough to succeed in team sports. By 1947, Joe Louis had been world heavyweight champion for ten consecutive years. Television was in its infancy, but millions of Americans still followed their favorite sports live on radio. When Louis won a prizefight, black fans spilled into the streets in a festive mood that lasted for hours. New fans followed the exploits of Jackie Robinson, who was voted National League Rookie of the Year in 1947. But still, white golf and tennis stars did not compete against blacks. Basketball did not have a national black star; the most celebrated black basketball players were Abe Saperstein's Harlem Globetrotters.

In 1948, Mike Duffey, the president of the NBL, asked the Rens to replace the Detroit Vagabond Kings. The new team was called the Dayton Rens, and it included Pop Gates, Dolly King, and George "Big Daddy" Crowe. (Crowe later played major-league baseball, and his brother Ray coached Oscar Robertson in high school.) The 1948 Rens also featured Nat "Sweetwater" Clifton and Jim Usry, who, years later, was elected mayor of Atlantic City, New Jersey. The team was no longer black-owned. None of the players wanted to play for Dayton, and Dayton fans had no interest in an all-black team. Their star player—Hank De Zonie, a former black college All-American at Clark College (Atlanta)—became ill.

This last version of the Rens won only 14 of 40 games. In the 1948 World Championship of Basketball, the Minneapolis Lakers beat the

The Globetrotters pose for a team photo. In the late 1940s, Saperstein's all-black independent team turned to "clown basketball," for which they became world-famous.

Rens in the finals 75-71. The Lakers were led by 6'10" George Mikan, the first big man to dominate pro basketball, who poured in 40 points in the championship game.

The Globetrotters were not as successful as the Rens in the World tournament. They had lost to the Renaissance 27-23 in the second round of the 1939 tourney but won the championship the following year by beating the NBL Chicago Bruins 31-19 in overtime. After their poor showing in the 1948 tournament, however, the Globetrotters concentrated on the clown basketball that they are famous for today. They performed comedy routines called reams. They used hidden-ball tricks in a pregame ritual known as the Magic Circle, and they interacted with fans, especially children. The Globetrotters almost never lost, whether to foreign teams, college all-stars, or the stooge teams (actually made up of talented former college players) they traveled with from the 1950s on. The black face of basketball during the NBL-BAA rivalry was the face of a clown.

Two of the best BAA teams were the New York Knickerbockers, led by Sonny Hertzberg, and the Washington Capitols, coached by ex–George Washington University star Arnold "Red" Auerbach. Like Hertzberg, Auerbach was a New Yorker. The Caps star was North Carolina's Horace "Bones" McKinney. Though the NBL had the more successful teams and a foothold in the Midwest, the BAA had the bigger arenas. When former Princeton star John "Bud" Palmer played his first game for the Knickerbockers, 17,000 fans packed Madison Square Garden. Washington was the BAA's Eastern Division champion in the inaugural season, but Philadelphia won the first league title. Jumpin' Joe Fulks, Matt Guokas Sr., and Howie Dallmar starred for Philadelphia.

Capital Roundball

Washington, D.C., also produced stellar black men's basketball teams. In the late 1930s and early 1940s, the Washington Lichtman Bears played such opponents as the Celtics and Rens in front of sellout crowds in Turner's Arena. Washington's best male players were from the Twelfth Street YMCA, where Dr. Edwin B. Henderson developed talented players.

The two leagues co-existed peacefully until Fort Wayne, Minneapolis, and Indianapolis decided to jump to the BAA because of the larger arenas in the East. This touched off the first threat of stars jumping leagues because of player-tampering by owners. NBL owners learned that Providence BAA owner Maurice Podoloff had convinced the three Midwestern teams to switch leagues. At an NBL meeting, a note was found that encouraged league owners to sign BAA players. When Podoloff found out about the note, he urged his BAA colleagues to lure players away from the NBL.

In May 1949, the graduating players of the University of Kentucky's team, who had formed the nucleus of the 1948 Olympic basketball team, announced they would enter the NBL intact as the Indianapolis Olympians. Player-signing wars had gotten out of control, and the NBL's franchises could not survive without their stars. With the big eastern gymnasiums, the BAA had the upper hand, and with better players they could fill the seats. In a peace agreement, the remaining financially secure BAA and NBL owners merged to form a new league that would begin play in the fall of 1949. The league would have Eastern, Central, and Western divisions. Regular seasons would consist of 62 games. Syracuse, Rochester, Minneapolis, Fort Wayne, Boston, and New York were among the charter members. The league was called the National Basketball Association.

CHAPTER 2

The Color Barrier Falls

There were 17 original NBA teams. The first season, 1949–50, was played without black players, although several teams played preliminary games against the Harlem Globetrotters to attract fans to NBA contests. The Trotters had a wider following and always outdrew the league teams in the doubleheaders. Many fans walked out before the NBA teams took the court for the second game. The league's only marquee, or star-quality, player in its inaugural season was the Minneapolis Lakers' bespectacled giant, George Mikan.

In an NBA Board of Governors meeting in 1949, the owners agreed by straw vote not to sign black players. This vote was not entirely inspired by racism, if at all. Owners feared that signing black players would upset Harlem Globetrotters owner Abe Saperstein, who employed basketball's premier black talents. Saperstein was the new league's most valuable asset because he filled arenas for the teams who could not attract fans on their own. So the league's hands-off policy toward black players seemed like a sensible business decision.

In 1950 the Knickerbockers owner, Ned Irish, desperately wanted to buy the contract of a Globetrotter player, Nat "Sweetwater" Clifton. A former Xavier All-American, the 6'5" pivot man was an excellent ball handler. Clifton, Reece "Goose" Tatum, and dribbling sensation Marques Haynes were the Globetrotters' most famous entertainers. NBA owners objected to Irish's interest in Clifton. Why make Saperstein angry? Irish threatened to pull his team from the league if he could not purchase Clifton's contract from the Trotters. He knew Madison Square Garden, the Knicks' home, was crucial to NBA success. The owners held an emergency straw vote, which was decided 6–5 in Irish's favor. (Six of the NBA's original 17 teams had folded by the 1950 season, reducing the league to 11 teams. The Washington Capitols would fold 35 games into the 1950–51 season.)

Maurice Podoloff was the first NBA commissioner, a five-footer who oversaw a game of giants. In the spring of 1950, Boston Celtics owner Walter Brown wanted to draft Duquesne University's Chuck Cooper, a black player. Brown knew that the Knicks were going to purchase the contract of Sweetwater Clifton for $10,000. Although the door was now open to sign black players, Brown knew that Cooper would be hesitant to sign with the unsteady new league. Cooper had already toured as a well-paid Harlem Globetrotter. Just as black players had previously not appealed to league owners, the NBA had little appeal to the best black ballplayers because the Globetrotters were paid better than even the best NBA players.

A Celtics scout informed Cooper that Boston was looking at him as a potential draft choice. Cooper was not surprised when Brown chose him with Boston second-round pick. Walter Brown had asked Haskell Cohen, a *Boston Globe* writer with ties to the Duquesne basketball program, to approach Chuck Cooper on behalf of Commissioner Podoloff. Through Cohen, the Celtics were able to draft Cooper, the NBA's first black draft choice, on April 25, 1950. Legend has it that when Walter Brown announced the selection of Chuck Cooper at the 1950 draft, a league official whispered to Brown, "Walt, Cooper's a colored boy." The Celtics signed Cooper for $7,500. In the same draft, Washington Capitols coach Bones McKinney selected West Virginia State's 6'6" Earl "Moon Fixer" Lloyd, a bruising black college All-American forward.

Coop

Chuck Cooper had graduated from Westchester High School in Pittsburgh, but he was not interested in playing basketball in college until he read about Long Island University's black star Dolly King in a few national magazines. Cooper considering enrolling at LIU because the team was coached by one of America's most respected basketball mentors, Clair Bee. He decided not to apply to the New York school, opting for West Virginia State instead. Cooper then enlisted in the U.S. Navy.

After serving a year and a half in the Navy, he remembered Clair Bee and the LIU program. He approached Duquesne University's basketball coach, Chuck Davies, to ask him to contact Bee for him. Bee offered him a scholarship on the advice of Brue Jackson, a black trainer for the Duquesne athletic teams and Pittsburgh Steelers. Cooper instead enrolled at Duquesne in his hometown of Pittsburgh. Duquesne had a long history of black basketball players, going back to Sol White at the turn of the century, but no black player had started there for years.

Because Duquesne had not recruited Cooper, he tried out and made the basketball squad as a walk-on. Cooper began his career at Duquesne University as a center. As a sophomore he had great leaping ability and could high jump 6'6", which was roughly his own height. Lean but muscular, Cooper possessed the grace of a gazelle. He was more of a scorer than a shooter.

Every time the team traveled south of the Mason-Dixon line, Cooper's presence made each contest the first racially integrated game at the host college. On December 23, 1946, University of Tennessee coach John Mauer refused to allow his Volunteers to play against Duquesne with Cooper. Tennessee was a member of the racially segregated Southern Conference. Two weeks later, Duquesne traveled to Miami for the outdoor Orange Bowl Basketball Tournament. On January 5, 1947, the University of Miami would not play its scheduled match against Duquesne, citing a Miami city law that forbade athletic competition between the races. When Cooper played against the University of Cincinnati, Bearcats players used racial slurs on the court. Three months later, former UCLA basketball star Jackie Robinson became the first black to play in a major-league baseball game.

Two years later when Cooper joined the Celtics, he had filled out to 220 pounds, and he was assigned a new position, strong forward. Although he had lost some of his elevation and quickness, he became a workman under the backboards. As a pro, Cooper was a steady defensive forward who lacked a scoring touch from long range. Most of his points came on power drives as a wing man when playmaker Bob Cousy set him up on the Celtics fast break. Cooper suffered chronic leg problems, ranging from knee injuries to muscle pulls. In his rookie season, Cooper gathered 562 rebounds, had 174 assists, and scored 615 points for a 9.3 per game average.

Neither fans nor NBA owners were impressed with the league's first black players. They were also a threat to business. When Celtics owner Walter Brown signed Cooper, Globetrotters' owner Abe Saperstein stormed into Brown's office in Boston Garden threatening never to schedule the popular Globetrotters in the Garden again. Though the clown team always boosted NBA attendance with their preliminary games, Brown did not back down. He was committed to Chuck Cooper, so he banned the Trotters from the Garden. The 1950–51 Celtics were 39–30, finishing second in the Eastern Division. Cooper averaged 8.2 points, and his scoring average dipped every season thereafter. After only averaging 3.3 points in 1954, he was dealt

Chuck Cooper, pictured here in 1953, was the first black player selected in the NBA draft. He played his first season with the Boston Celtics in 1950. Although mostly unknown today, Cooper, Nat Clifton, and Earl Lloyd were the Jackie Robinsons of the NBA.

to Milwaukee, where he averaged 8.2 points in 1954–55. Cooper spent his final NBA season with the Fort Wayne Pistons in 1956.

Cooper had actually played for the Globetrotters before reporting to the Celtics, but he didn't like the second-rate hotels the Trotters stayed in during their U.S. tours. Cooper never saw himself as a pioneer. He considered Jackie Robinson the trailblazer for blacks in professional team sports. While he played in the NBA, Cooper had to stay in separate hotels when his teams visited Baltimore and Washington. Accommodations for black NBA players did not begin to change until the late 1950s, when Elgin Baylor and Bill Russell were stars.

After six years in the NBA, Cooper signed with the Harlem Magicians, a team fashioned after the Globetrotters. The pay was good, but an auto accident shortened his career. Cooper became active in the parks and recreation system in Pittsburgh. In 1976 he was inducted into the Basketball Hall of Fame.

Sweets

Like Chuck Cooper, Sweetwater Clifton switched from center to forward as an NBA player. Nathaniel Clifton was born in Little Rock, Arkansas, but his family moved to Chicago when he was five years old. Like millions of black Americans before the Great Depression, the Clifton family left the segregated South for the economic opportunity of the industrial North. From 1900 to 1930 the black population of Chicago grew from 44,000 to 233,000. In the 1930s, Chicago had only two public high schools for blacks. Wendell Phillips, with an enrollment of 3,000, was one of them. During the 1930s Clifton attended Phillips High with future *Ebony* magazine publisher John H. Johnson and John Sanford, who became comedian Redd Foxx.

In high school Clifton was Chicago's best center. At 6'5", he shot with accuracy and handled the ball well. After an outstanding high school career, he went to Xavier College in New Orleans, where teams led by stars from Phillips High had lost only two games between 1935

During a 1955 Knicks-Celtics game, Nat "Sweetwater" Clifton tries to outrace Boston's Bob Cousy to a loose ball. The 29-year-old player had starred for the Rens and Globetrotters when he signed with the NBA's Knicks in 1950.

and 1938. Xavier was so good that the world's best pro basketball team, the Harlem Rens, beat them by only one point, 38–37, in a game.

Nat Clifton improved his basketball skills in college. He was a very popular player, with unusual habits. He always took a shower at halftime. He wore too much cologne before he went out for an evening. Because he could drink a 12-pack of soda at a time, his teammates nicknamed him Sweetwater. After a career as an All-Southern Conference center, Clifton enlisted in the U.S. Army, where he played service basketball for three years. In 1947, he played briefly with the Dayton Metropolitans, then with the Harlem Rens. He signed with the Harlem Globetrotters. By 1949, the man the other Trotters called Sweets was one of the two stars of the traveling unit. New York Knicks owner Ned Irish thought Clifton would be a crowd pleaser in Madison Square Garden, and a good player as well.

Clifton was past his prime when the Knicks signed him. Most 29-year-old basketball players have a few good years left. Clifton was that age as a rookie, and he was an old 29, worn down by the years of service ball and Globetrotters travel. He relied more on skills than athleticism. Clifton could dribble better than almost any NBA big man of his day, and few players of any size were better passers. Sweets set strong picks, or screens, for other players, and his long arms made him an excellent defender and rebounder. He was very careful not to use the basketball tricks he had learned with the Trotters. NBA coaches frowned on showy moves, and opponents didn't like to be embarrassed. The flashiest NBA player during Clifton's career was a white player, Boston guard Bob Cousy.

Sweets played in 65 games as a Knicks rookie, averaging 8.6 points, dishing out 162 assists, and snatching 491 rebounds. He averaged 10.6 points in both the 1951–52 and 1952–53 seasons, two years in which the Knicks reached the NBA finals. In 1955, at age 33, he averaged a career high 13.1 points. He finished his career with the 1958 Detroit Pistons. Sweets played in 53 playoff games and one All-Star game and posted career averages of 10.0 points and 8.2 rebounds per game.

Earl "Big Cat" Lloyd snatches a rebound in a 1955 game. On October 31, 1950, Lloyd became the first black man to play in a NBA game.

Big Cat

After a stellar schoolboy career at Parker-Gray High School in Alexandria, Virginia, Earl Lloyd enrolled at a black college, West Virginia State. There he earned the nickname Moon Fixer because he could jump so high. Lloyd is still considered one of the greatest black college basketball players ever. His strength was legendary. The NBA

41

Washington Capitols selected him with their ninth pick in the 1950 draft. On Halloween, 1950, Earl Lloyd played in the Capitols' 78–70 loss to Rochester, the first time a black man had played in an NBA game. (Washington had cut its other black draft choice, Harold "Wildman" Hunter of North Carolina College.) Lloyd only played seven games before his Washington team folded.

Lloyd, now nicknamed Big Cat, had 444 rebounds for the Syracuse Nationals in the 1952–53 season, 529 in 1953–54, and 529 again in 1954–55, when the Nationals won the NBA championship. His best scoring mark was 10.2 points a game (1954–55). In 1958 he was traded to Detroit. In nine NBA seasons, Lloyd averaged 8.4 points and 6.4 rebounds during the regular season and 8.1 points and 5.8 rebounds in 44 playoff games. He coached the Pistons in the 1970s. Many more Americans can name the first black major-league baseball player, Jackie Robinson, than can name the first black player to participate in an NBA game, Earl Lloyd.

CHAPTER 3

Giant Steps

In the mid-1940s, George Mikan was a freshman at DePaul University in Chicago. Although he stood 6'10", he had been refused a basketball scholarship to Notre Dame. The freshman, who wore thick glasses like a giant Clark Kent, joined a Catholic Youth Organization team to sharpen his skills. One of his opponents was Sweetwater Clifton. Under the guidance of a new DePaul coach, Ray Meyer, Mikan became the first man his size to be a major college basketball star. He continued his stardom as a professional, leading his Minneapolis Lakers teams to four NBA titles in five years (1950, 1952–54). As good as Mikan was—career regular season averages of 23.1 points and 13.4 rebounds a game—he was not very agile.

The NBA's First Black Big Men

Walter Dukes and Ray Felix were the NBA's first two black giants. (Physicians consider men over 6'6" giants, and in the 1950s, the average American male stood only 5'8".) Dukes stood 7' tall. He played college ball at Seton Hall University. Though Dukes arrived on campus as an uncoordinated beanpole, he was transformed into an All-American by his coach, former St. John's star Honey Russell. In 1952, Seton Hall won 25 of 27 games and ran off 27 victories in a row. Dukes, a senior, was the MVP of the National Invitation Tournament (NIT) tournament, which Seton Hall won over St. John's. (In those days, the NIT crown was more coveted than the NCAA championship.) Dukes, who was the first giant of his race to star for a major college basketball team, averaged an amazing 33 rebounds per game as a senior.

As a pro, Dukes spent his rookie year with the Knicks, but he blossomed in his second season, averaging 10.1 points and 11.2 rebounds a game for the 1956–57 Lakers. The Lakers traded him to the Detroit Pistons, and Dukes played six more years in the NBA. He averaged 13.0 rebounds for the 1958 Pistons, a team featuring Sweetwater Clifton. Dukes's best year came in 1959–60, when he averaged 15.2 points and 13.4 rebounds with the Pistons. He played in 35 playoff games and 2 All-Star contests.

Ray Felix played only one year at Long Island University before a betting scandal rocked the LIU basketball program. Though Felix stood 6'10", he was slender and not very aggressive. He had a productive rookie season with the Baltimore Bullets and was named the 1954 Rookie of the Year. Felix was the league's fourth leading rebounder in 1953–54, averaging more than 13.3 boards a game. In 1954–55, playing for the Knicks, he was the fifth-best rebounder and fourth-best field-goal shooter. Between 1956 and 1958, Felix averaged slightly more than 12 points a game for New York. He finished his career with the Los Angeles Lakers in 1961–62. He played in 38 playoff games and 1 All-Star contest.

Although Dukes and Felix had solid pro careers, the greatest black big men were waiting in the wings.

Seven-footer Walter Dukes was the first black big man to play in the NBA. He started his eight-year career with the Knicks in 1955.

Bill Russell

William Felton Russell was born into poverty in Monroe, Louisiana, in 1934. Bill's father worked odd jobs—moving and hauling, iron-making, and logrolling. (Logrolling was how land was cleared before people used bulldozers.) His grandfather was a proud man who had stood up to the Ku Klux Klan when they threatened to take his land in 1917.

When Bill was eight, his family moved to West Oakland, California, to escape southern racism and seek better employment opportunities. As a boy Bill spent hours in the Oakland Public Library. His favorite historical figure was Henri Christophe, a leader of the Haitian struggle for independence. Bill was fascinated with books that depicted foreign marvels, such as the Seven Wonders of the Ancient World. He found science and magic interesting. He took home prints by Leonardo DaVinci and Michelangelo, rolling them up so other kids wouldn't know what they were. Inspired by the artwork, Bill tried painting for a while.

Bill's older brother Charlie was one of Oakland's best high school athletes. In tenth grade at McClymonds High Bill tried out for basketball. The coach was a white teacher named George Powles, who knew very little about the game. Bill was tall but uncoordinated. He tried to make the high school football team as a defensive end and was cut. As is the case with many tall youngsters, his growth had outpaced his agility. Rather than cut Russell from the school team, Powles kept 16 players, and the least talented two, Russell and a boy named Roland Campbell, shared a uniform. When Roland wore the singlet and shorts, Bill sat up in the bleachers, and vice versa.

Powles was a concerned teacher. He warned his players to avoid roughness on the court and not to be goaded into violence, because newspapers would call a fracas involving white players a scuffle and one with black players a riot. Powles took a special interest in Russell, probably foreseeing a scholarship for his lanky substitute if he could

46

improve his game. He gave Bill two dollars to join the Boys Club, where he could play against different competition.

In 1952, a California All-Star tour for high school players was organized by the Jaycees Club and the Mohawk Club. The sponsors wanted a player from McClymonds High. Bill Russell was not all-anything, not even honorable mention All-Oakland Athletic League, although there were only six teams in the Oakland high school league. But McClymonds had a strong sports reputation: Russell's high school mates Vada Pinson, Curt Flood, and Frank Robinson became major-league baseball all-stars in the 1960s. Russell was selected to play on the high school team of stars.

The California All-Stars played teams in Northern California, Oregon, and Washington and in the Territory of British Columbia and other parts of Canada. Competing against older players, the team played Western Washington College and the University of British Columbia. Russell, who had only read about the beauty of nature in the Oakland Public Library, finally saw such impressive sights as the Cascade Mountains. At the end of the tour, Russell was a better, more confident athlete. Without Powles's interest in Russell and the California All-Star tour, basketball fans would never have heard of Bill Russell.

After graduating from high school, Bill took a job in the San Francisco naval shipyards, where he worked as a sheet-metal carrier. An alumni booster for the University of San Francisco, Hal De Julio, saw Bill working and remembered having seen him play well against an Oakland schoolboy star named Truman Bruce. De Julio suggested that Russell apply to the University of San Francisco (USF), but Bill had never heard of the small Catholic school. Bill decided to give college a shot.

Russell was not the only USF basketball player who matriculated under unusual circumstances. In 1951, a young man named K. C. Jones had broken the AAA high school scoring record in San Francisco at Commerce High. Jones wanted to get a postal service job after graduation because postal service workers had good job security and could afford to drive late-model cars. Although a superb athlete, Jones had received no college scholarship offers until a reporter published a story that K. C. was being recruited by UCLA, California-Berkeley, Stanford, and Washington. New USF coach Phil Woolpert read the story, sought out the local prospect, and offered him a scholarship. In Jones's freshman year (1952), the Dons had their third straight losing season.

In 1953, with Russell developing as an effective pivot man on the freshman team, USF came within one game of finishing at .500. Coach Woolpert stressed defensive play, which both Russell and Jones were suited for. The 6'1" Jones had quick feet, a strong lower body, and a tenacious streak. The 6'9" Russell could high jump his own height, was left handed (which surprised shooters even when they knew it, because his blocked shots seemed to come out of nowhere), and he could run the floor like a guard. On the track team Bill high jumped 6'8" when the world record was 6'11". The university president praised his high-jump effort and urged him to break the world record because the publicity would be good for the college. Russell stifled an impulse to laugh; he had just taken up the event. He would soon put USF on the national map, but not through his high jumping.

In 1954, USF opened against California. Russell swatted the first shot by Berkeley's big man, Bob McKeen. On the sidelines, Cal's legendary coach Pete Newell said, "Now where in the world did he come from?" It is not clear whether Newell was referring to Russell's recruitment or his position on the court. Either way, Russell had made his presence known, and he rejected 12 shots in his coming-out party, outscoring Bob McKeen 23-14 as USF upset Cal.

The Dons' jubilation was short lived, however. Before their second game, K. C. Jones suffered a ruptured appendix, which put him out of the lineup for the season. The conference voted to extend Jones's college eligibility by an extra year. The 1954 Dons finished a respectable 14–7 without their playmaker.

College Championships

In the 1955 season opener, the Dons played Chico State, and Russell toyed with the 6'1" center assigned to guard him. The Dons also beat Loyola of Los Angeles that weekend, while UCLA thrashed Santa Clara 75–35. USF's next game was a road match against UCLA at Pauley Pavilion in Westwood. UCLA was ranked No. 8 nationally. Even the ever-confident K. C. Jones expected the Bruins to win by 20 or 25 points. The game, however, turned out to be a battle. Jones shot down UCLA All-American Maury Taft, and Russell played well against 6'5" Willie "The Whale" Naulls. The Dons lost a squeaker, 47–40.

The close defeat boosted the Dons' confidence about their capabilities. At a big tournament in Oklahoma City, fans taunted them during their practice session. The court in Oklahoma City was elevated like a stage, with the seats below it. Racist spectators shouted "Globetrotters!" at the Dons, who had six black players. Pennies were thrown at them. Perhaps for luck, Bill Russell collected the scattered coins and gave them to coach Woolpert.

In the tournament opener against top seed Wichita State the next evening, USF jumped out to a 25–3 lead. The Dons blew out Wichita State, Oklahoma City, and George Washington, three excellent teams. Russell was named tournament most valuable player.

Led by speedy guards K. C. Jones and Hal Perry and the intimidator Russell, USF ran their record to 23–1 before making it to the NCAA West Regionals. In the first round of the regionals, they routed West Texas State 89–66. In the semis, they turned back a fast-breaking Utah squad, holding them 20 points under their scoring average in a 78-59 win.

The Western Regional Final pitted USF against Beavers of Oregon State University, a team starring 7'3" Swede Halbrook and 6'6" Tony Vlastelica. The game marked the beginning of a Russell tradition. The Dons' center had a nervous stomach and vomited before the contest. Years later, that habit became a Boston Celtics good luck charm because it signified that Russell was ready to play.

Vlastelica and Halbrook sandwiched Russell, making things difficult for the Dons. They led by only a basket with 13 seconds remaining. During a Beavers time-out, Jones left the USF huddle before the break was over, but then Woolpert summoned him back for a last instruction. OSU's Jim O'Toole, the player defending Jones, blocked K. C.'s return to the team bench. Jones tried to go around O'Toole, but the Beaver moved into his path. K. C. pushed O'Toole and continued toward his bench. A referee called a technical foul on Jones. An OSU shooter sank the free toss, and OSU was awarded the basketball at halfcourt. Now USF's lead was only one. State inbounded the ball crosscourt, then into the favorite shooting corner of guard Ron Robins. Robins released his shot as the hearts of USF rooters froze. Time seemed suspended in slow motion. The effort caromed off the rear rim, straight up, and Swede Halbrook and K. C. Jones shared the rebound. A jump ball was ruled. The towering Halbrook easily won the toss, but he tapped the ball to the Dons' Hal Perry. Players surrounded Perry, who raced to advance the ball over the ten-second midcourt line. A Beavers player actually managed to free the ball from Perry, but the ensuing OSU layup occurred after the final whistle. The Dons were headed for the Final Four in Kansas City.

In the NCAA semifinals, the Dons beat the Colorado Buffaloes 62-50, which set up a final against the defending champions, the La Salle Explorers from Philadelphia. La Salle starred Tom Gola, a 6' 7" swingman generally considered the nation's best player. Gola not only was the 1954 NCAA tourney MVP (with 114 points in five games) but was considered by some sportswriters to be the best college basketball player ever. Gola was quick, owned a deadly shot, and had good instincts and sure hands. In the Dons' team meeting before the championship, coach Woolpert surprised his team by picking 6'1" K. C. Jones, not Bill Russell, to shadow Gola. Woolpert's strategy was to let the ball-hawking guard chase the All-American Gola while Rus-

*University of San Francisco center Bill Russell
demonstrates his form on a layup. Led by Russell, the Dons
won back-to-back NCAA championships (1955, 1956).*

USF's K. C. Jones drives past a Cal player during the
1955–56 season. The ball-hawking guard was a superb
defender and would later be a standout as an NBA
player and coach.

sell stayed closer to the basket to ward off any drives. If Gola eluded Jones, Russell would be there to clean up the mistakes.

It was a masterpiece of defensive tactics as Gola scored only six baskets and four free throws. Even Jones outscored him, ringing up 24 points. Russell contributed 23 points as USF won the national championship 77-63. Bill was named tournament MVP.

In the off-season, NCAA officials brainstormed methods of limiting Russell's effectiveness. They discussed stronger rules concerning offensive and defensive goaltending. What emerged from the rules meetings was a vote to double the width of the foul lane from 6 feet to 12 feet. Post players could set up in the free throw lane only for three seconds at a time. By making the violation area twice its previous size, the new rule would move big men out from under the hoop. The change was nicknamed the Russell Rule.

USF had a stronger schedule and the Russell Rule to contend with in 1955. Every college team would be gunning for the Dons. USF won seven games before traveling east to the nation's biggest Christmas tournament, Madison Square Garden's Holiday Festival. The first game was a grudge match between La Salle and USF. Although Tom Gola had graduated and was playing with the NBA Warriors, La Salle still led 45–43 four minutes into the second half. Russell began asserting himself on both ends of the court. Despite a fine effort by the Explorers' Alonzo Lewis, USF won going away 79-62, buoyed by Russell's 26 points, 22 boards, and 12 blocked shots.

In the tournament semifinal, Holy Cross, led by 6' 8" gunner Tommy Heinsohn, was ahead of USF at intermission 32-29. USF rebounded again, riding Russell's 24 points and 24 rebounds to a 67-51 victory. The Festival finals featured two western teams, much to the dismay of Garden rooters. USF defeated a strong UCLA team, starring All-Americans Willie Naulls and Maury Taft, 70-53. In what was becoming routine, Russell won tourney MVP laurels.

The Dons were unstoppable. With Russell triggering fast breaks with either blocked shots or rebounds, they moved the ball around swiftly and shot well. On defense, the Dons knew that they could gamble because Big Russ was hovering near the basket awaiting any drives into the lane. The Russell Rule didn't stop USF, and it actually hindered Russell's offensive opponents, prohibiting them from camping out close to their own baskets.

The Dons set their sights on LIU's NCAA record of 39 consecutive victories. The streak stood at 38 when USF met Cal. Pete Newell, Cal's coach, was known as a master strategist. He devised a plan to lure Russell away from the lane. He put his backup center, Joe Haggler, at the point near midcourt with instructions to hold the ball under one arm. Russell strayed no farther than the free throw line, refusing to take the bait. Cal held the ball for eight long minutes. The strategy led not to a victory, just a lower score: USF 33, Cal 24. (There was no shot clock in men's college basketball until the mid-1980s.)

The streak continued. The Dons beat SMU, a team with its own 19-game victory string and 6'8" star center Jim Krebs. Elsewhere, Iowa, led by Carl "Sugar" Cain, was putting together a 17-game win streak. Cain dropped 34 points on perennial power Kentucky in the Hawkeyes' 89-77 elimination of the Wildcats in the Regional Final. USF knocked Temple and their star Hal "King" Lear out of the championship tournament with a six-point victory.

In the title game Cain sneaked around the baseline for several backdoor hoops to put Iowa up 15-4. Coach Woolpert switched Gene Brown to guard Sugar. K. C. Jones was watching the game in street clothes because his extra year of eligibility did not include the NCAA tournament. Brown was effective on Cain, and USF passed Iowa at 24-23, then surged ahead 38-33 at halftime. The Dons controlled the second half and cruised to their second straight college crown, 83-71. Russell had rejected 12 shots, grabbed 27 rebounds, and scored 26 points. One Final Four custom, however, was broken. Temple's Hal Lear was named tournament MVP, ostensibly for his unprecedented 160 points in five games during the tournament. Very seldom is a player not involved in the final game named MVP of the college championship. (It did not occur again for ten years.) Russell had been named MVP of five straight tournaments. His team had won 55 games in a row.

Gold and Green

The 1956 NBA player draft was the most intriguing in the league's first decade. The NBA franchise that drafted Bill Russell would be without his services the first two months of the NBA season because he was a member of the U.S. Olympic basketball team. The 1956 Summer Olympics were being held in Melbourne, Australia, the first time the games were ever played south of the equator. The games were scheduled much later than usual—November 22 to December 11—because the seasons in the Southern Hemisphere are the reverse of what they are in the Northern Hemisphere.

The Harlem Globetrotters reportedly made a $50,000 offer to Russell. The Trotters' actual offer was probably closer to the $17,000 bonus they had paid in 1953 to Walter Dukes, the 7-footer who had led Seton Hall to an undefeated season as a senior. After a two-year stint with the Globies, some NBA watchers thought Dukes adopted bad habits that stunted his development as an NBA center. As Russell weighed his options, the league owners with the top draft selections pondered theirs. How much money should they offer a man who was bound for a long Olympic exhibition tour and then the Melbourne Games? There were other factors. Russell appeared frail, though he was deceptively strong. He scored primarily from inside and had not displayed any shooting range. Could he score against pro centers? Why select a young man who might follow Walter Dukes's lead and sign with the high-paying Harlem Globetrotters? Some NBA owners simply had not seen Russell play, as televised college basketball games were rare. Most players were scouted via hoop magazines; a player actually witnessed in game films or movie newsreels was a rarity.

The Rochester Royals had the first pick, followed by the St. Louis Hawks and the Minneapolis Lakers. Rochester owner Lester Harrison could not afford the $25,000 Russell wanted. The Royals already had a good young pivot man, 1956 Rookie of the Year Maurice Stokes. St. Louis also had a promising new big man, 6'9" Bob Pettit, and team owner Ben Kerner was short on cash. St. Louis also was a very segregated city where the best restaurants and hotels were for whites only. Minneapolis was seeking a center to replace the legendary George Mikan. The Boston Celtics sorely needed a rebounder to trigger the team's legendary fast break, but they had the sixth pick.

Celtics coach Red Auerbach called Ben Kerner. He offered his own center, "Easy" Ed Macauley, for the rights to draft Russell. Auerbach pointed to Macauley's appeal for Hawks fans: The center had played at St. Louis University. Easy Ed was more of a finesse player than a physical type, and Auerbach desperately wanted a superior rebounder. No one knew that Russell had decided that if he was chosen by the Lakers, he would not play there. Kerner needed Macauley to draw fans, and Bob Pettit was already doing a good job on the backboards for the Hawks.

Macauley was closer to the end of his career than Auerbach let on, and he had been ill. Easy Ed was even homesick for St. Louis. Kerner became a bit suspicious of Auerbach's eagerness to deal the 6'10" shooter, and instinct moved him to ask for one more player. He asked the Boston coach to include Cliff Hagan, a 6'4" rookie who had been an All-American at Kentucky before entering the military. Auerbach wanted the shot-blocking Russell enough to throw in the promising young player. Although Red would not be able to work with his first choice until Russell returned from the Olympics, Boston had a territorial draft selection, which they planned to use for Holy Cross's 6' 8" Tommy Heinsohn. Auerbach thought his team could get by with their 6'10" center Arnie Risen until Russell arrived.

By December 5, when Russell left Australia to marry Rose Swisher, the daughter of his high school counselor, the Celts were 13–3 and enjoyed a five-game lead in the Eastern Division. Guard Bob Cousy's ball wizardry set up sharpshooters Bill Sharman and

Tommy Heinsohn with ideal shots. The addition of Russell would give the Boston team more possessions off rebounds and rejected shots and allow Cousy to execute the fast break.

Russell reported to the Celtics on December 22. In Melbourne, he, Carl Cain, and K. C. Jones had led a U.S. team that captured the gold medal, winning every game by at least 30 points. The rookie joined a Celtics team that had raced to a 16–8 record. In one of basketball's little ironies, the opponent in Russell's first game was St. Louis, the team from which Auerbach had secured his draft rights. In only 21 minutes, Russell collected 16 rebounds, and Boston won 95-93. He was not in peak condition because the Melbourne experience had drained him. Russell was also unfamiliar with his teammates. His strengths were his leaping ability, combined with uncanny timing and strength. He threw a great outlet pass. Shooters feared him, which changed the Boston defense. Cousy and Sharman were not particularly talented defenders, but now they could funnel their men toward Russell.

Unlike most centers, Bill Russell was a student of the game. At USF he and K. C. Jones barely spoke to each other for the first month after they met. When they became roommates, however, Jones began to tell Russell, little by little, his theories and observations about basketball. Jones had noticed that every individual had a finite field of vision, with blind spots on either side. During a game, he told Russell, an offensive player with his head down had no peripheral vision. A player dribbling with his right hand had limited vision to the left. Jones knew how to position himself for a steal based on these distances and lines of sight.

Russell told Jones that he had noticed that 75 percent of rebounds are taken below the rim, so a horizontal advantage was more important than a vertical one. He had broken the court up into geometric areas, and he knew opponents often forgot he was left-handed, which facilitated much of his shot blocking. After a few skull sessions about the science of basketball, K. C. and Bill called themselves "Ein-

*Bill Russell won 11 NBA championships in his
13-year career. In his last three years with the Boston Celtics,
he served as the team's player-coach.*

steins in sneakers." In their free time, they walked paces apart, telling one another when each had left the other's field of vision. This enhanced their awareness of activity on the court and of what their opponents could and could not see.

A month after Russell's first game, Boston had sank to 24–24, even though on January 4 former Kentucky All-American Frank Ramsey rejoined the team after military service. Now, they led Philadelphia by only 3½ games and New York by 4. They turned things around, winning eight straight, and The team went on to a 44–28 mark, finishing 6 games ahead of the surging Syracuse Nationals. Every Eastern team finished above .500. Every Western squad lost more than it won, with three teams tied for first at 34–38.

The 1957 NBA Playoffs

In the Eastern Finals, Boston eliminated Syracuse in three games, and St. Louis likewise swept Minneapolis in the Western Finals. Boston had beaten the Hawks in seven of nine regular-season games. Basketball fans and sportswriters looked forward to the Hawks-Celtics matchup. Fans wondered whether Russell could stop Hawks big man Bob Pettit, a fine scorer and rebounder out of LSU. The series would also determine the wisdom or folly in Ben Kerner's trade of the Russell draft pick. In Russell's mind there were no two ways about it. He could have never played for St. Louis. He played well against the Hawks as a rookie in Kiel Auditorium, but bigots in the stands yelled "gorilla" and "black baboon" at the young center. Bill hoped to silence the bleacher bums in the league finals. St. Louis was an all-white team with a very talented front court: Easy Ed Macauley, Charlie Share, and Cliff Hagan.

The first game went into double overtime. Led by Bob Pettit's 37 points, the Hawks triumphed 125-123. Boston won game two easily, 114-99. The series moved to St. Louis, Russell's least favorite arena. At Kiel Auditorium the Hawks came out on top in another close contest, 100-98. Up against the wall in game four, the Celts recouped for a 123-118 win to even the series at 2–2.

Boston took game five in the Garden by a decisive 124-109 margin. Auerbach's men were one game away from a world title. Two days later, a buzzer beater by Cliff Hagan in St. Louis sealed a 96-94 Hawks win, knotting the series at three-all. It had been a tough series. Cousy was passing like a magician, and Heinsohn and Sharman were nailing long shots. Pettit and Russell tussled under the backboards, fighting for every rebound. The final game was held on Saturday, April 13. Boston surged to big leads on six occasions, but St. Louis closed the gap each time. With 13 seconds remaining, Cousy made a foul shot to put Boston ahead 103-101. What else could happen? Would Kerner or Auerbach emerge the genius?

Bob Pettit was fouled. The 6'9" Louisianan coolly netted both free throws, sending the deciding game into overtime. The players had played their hearts out, and now they were being asked to give more. In the extra period, the Hawks converted a basket with no time left to make it 113-113. Double OT.

Russell had been in big pressure games before. He had played on back-to-back NCAA champions for a racially mixed team that every school gunned at. Overseas, he had led the U.S. Olympic team to a gold medal. He had faced stiff competition in major track meets as a high jumper. With a minute and a half to play in the second overtime, Boston had a 122-121 edge. Med Park drove for a basket, and Russell rejected his shot, sparking a Boston fast break. Frank Ramsey pulled up and drilled a jump shot. 124-121 Boston.

The final 1:12 took about ten minutes to play, due to fouls, substitutions, and scuffles for loose balls. St. Louis narrowed the lead to 124–123. With two seconds left, Boston's strongman James "Jungle Jim" Loscotoff was fouled. Loscotoff made it 125-123 by hitting one free throw. Time-out. The Hawks huddled around coach Alex Hannum, who drew up a play that called for the Hawks to try to hit their backboard with a long throw. (The clock would not tick until a St.

Louis player or Celtic touched the ball). Hannum hoped Bob Pettit could catch the carom—which would surprise the Celtics—and score.

The players took their positions. The Hawks heaved the ball toward the opposite backboard. The rebound off the glass came to Pettit, who put up a shot. It bounced off the rim. Boston celebrated its first NBA championship. Bill Russell had gone from the college title to a professional crown in a year, with Olympic gold in between. Because of his shortened season, Russell was not named rookie of the year. That honor went to his teammate Tommy Heinsohn, whose shooting prowess earned him the machine-gun nickname Ack Ack.

First Full Season

After his rookie season in the NBA, Bill Russell was already the league's premier black center. In 1957–58, he led the Celtics in minutes played and shooting percentage and the league in rebounding at 22.7 per game. He was named league MVP but somehow was left off the All-league first team, an oversight that bothered him for years. Boston finished 49–23, handily winning the East and breezing through a 4 games to 1 Eastern playoffs victory over Philadelphia. The Hawks won the Western Finals by an identical 4–1 margin over Detroit.

The Boston–St. Louis finals rematch was tied one apiece when Russell injured his ankle in game three. The Hawks won the game 111–108. The absence of Russell was not felt immediately as the Celtics evened the series with a 109-98 win in game four. St. Louis took a one-game lead by winning the next game 102-100, and the series moved back to St. Louis, where the Hawks could clinch a title with a win.

Russell tested the ankle, but he was ineffective. Auerbach took him out so Russell wouldn't aggravate the injury. Without Russell to contend with, Bob Pettit scored 19 of the Hawks' last 21 points, giving him 50 for the game. The Hawks eked out a hard-fought win, 110-109. NBA fans now realized how valuable Russell was.

The Dynasty Begins

In 1958–59, St. Louis and Boston again won their divisions easily. Boston still had Bill Sharman, who shot .932 from the foul line, and Bob Cousy, who won his ninth straight league assists title. Russell again led Boston in minutes and field-goal accuracy and the entire league in rebounds, averaging 23.0. Boston finished 57–20, St. Louis 49–23.

St. Louis unexpectedly did not make it to the 1959 NBA finals. To the disappointment of league officials and television executives who looked forward to a Hawks-Celtics rematch, NBA Rookie of the Year Elgin Baylor led the Lakers to a 4–2 Western Finals triumph over Pettit's Hawks. Boston had beaten Minneapolis 18 straight times before the 1959 NBA finals, and the playoffs would be no different. With Cousy, Russell, Heinsohn, and a new black player, Sam Jones, Boston swept to their second title, 4–0. Russell now had two championship rings.

A New Rival

The 1959 off-season was marked by the Philadelphia Warriors' signing of the one player that the world thought could challenge Bill Russell: 7'1" former Kansas All-American Wilton "Wilt the Stilt" Chamberlain. Wilt and Bill had a lot in common. Both had been college high jumpers. Both could run the floor, and their wiry frames belied their strength. Both young men were intimidators who liked to psyche out the opposition. Russell had had a tremendous impact on the NBA. His shot-blocking ability, for example, rendered three-time league scoring champion Neil Johnston ineffective at age 30. The 6'8" hook shot artist retired three years after Russell joined the league.

There were, however, significant differences between the two giants. Wilt had been recruited by 227 colleges; Russell was working

Wilt Chamberlain skies to grab a rebound against the Pistons. The Big Dipper was the greatest offensive player in NBA history.

in a shipyard when a USF booster approached him about attending college. Russell was a late bloomer, but Wilt had been on YMCA and church championship teams as a teen, and he had once scored 92 points in a high school game. Russell was a two-time NCAA champion; Chamberlain's Kansas squad lost the 1957 NCAA Final. Finally, Russell had turned the Globetrotters down, whereas Wilt played with them. Standing 7'1" and weighing 245 pounds as a rookie, Chamberlain was bigger than Russell (6'9", 220). Their athleticism put them ahead of other centers. Immediately, Chamberlain signed for $65,000 more than Bill Russell and Bob Cousy combined.

The Minister of Defense

K. C. Jones's defensive style influenced the generations of guards that followed him: Walt "Clyde" Frazier, Alvin Robertson, Don "Slick" Watts, Ron Lee, Lafayette "Fat" Lever, Dennis Johnson, and Gary Payton. All the players who like to get in their opponents' jerseys

The tall titans first met on November 7, 1959. Russell was aware of all the pregame hype and knew that for the rest of his career he would be measured against Chamberlain. He reminded himself that basketball was a team game, not a contest between individuals. In that first Russell-Chamberlain battle, Russell grabbed 35 rebounds to Chamberlain's 28. He held the highly publicized 7-footer to only 12 baskets in 38 attempts, and Boston won the game.

The Celtics were even better in 1959–60. Russell's old USF buddy K. C. Jones joined the team after two years of military service. Jones was so skilled a defender that the Los Angeles Rams had drafted him as a defensive back even though he had not played college football. K. C. Jones and Sam Jones were backup guards for veterans Cousy and Sharman. Russell's backup was a 6'8" Boston Red Sox pitcher, Eugene "Jumping Gene" Conley. Russell averaged 24.0 rebounds that season, second to Chamberlain's 26.8.

The Celtics won the East with a 59–16 record. Chamberlain's Philly squad was 10 games behind at 49–26. St. Louis won the West, and Boston and St. Louis advanced to another grudge match in the NBA finals. Boston took the seven-game series in a 122-103 final—Russell's third title in four seasons. The Celtics' domination of the NBA was based on tough defenders—such as Russell and K. C. Jones, who forced turnovers—and Russell's rebounding dominance, which frustrated everyone but Wilt. It was common for Boston to outscore opponents 24–6 or 16–3 in runs triggered by blocked shots and steals. The Celtics defense gave them more possessions of the basketball, which meant more opportunities to score. Yet neither steals nor blocked shots statistics were kept by the league until 1973.

Wilt Chamberlain, Elgin Baylor, and the Cincinnati Royals' highly touted rookie Oscar "The Big O" Robertson all averaged 30 points or more in 1960–61. Boston finished with a record of 57–22. Despite Chamberlain's 38.4 scoring average, the Warriors finished 11 games back in the East. St. Louis won 51 games to capture the West, and Robertson's Royals won 14 more games than the previous season and still finished in last place in the West. Elgin Baylor poured in 71 points in a November game against New York. Bill Russell averaged 23.9 rebounds, and Chamberlain pulled in 27.2 a game. In the 1961 NBA finals, the Hawks, fatigued from a seven-game Western final with Los Angeles, succumbed to Boston 4–1. It was Russell's fourth championship.

Filling It Up

NBA basketball was played at a faster pace than ever during the 1960-61 season. Making full use of the 24-second clock, teams averaged a record 118 points a game. Three years earlier, the average score was 106.6; three seasons before that it had been only 93.1. Elgin Baylor, Bob Pettit, Wilt Chamberlain, and Oscar Robertson ushered the game into a new era. Three of those players were black.

A Season to Remember

Two basketball hierarchies had emerged in the NBA: the Celtics as a team and Wilt Chamberlain as an individual. Boston continued its domination in the 1961–62 season, posting an impressive 60–20 record. Wilt Chamberlain, however, was the talk of the league. The Big Dipper scored 40 or more points in 14 games in a row in December. He put together streaks of seven, six, and five games (twice) in which he scored at least 50 points. On March 2, 1962, he went off the charts with a 100-point game against the Knicks. Chamberlain averaged 50.4 points in 1961–62 (which is still a record—one that is unlikely to be broken) to go with his league-leading 3,882 minutes and more than 2,000 rebounds for a 25.7 average. Sportswriters and opposing coaches called Chamberlain selfish and pinned the loser label on him. Despite his Herculean stats, the Warriors finished 11 games behind Boston in the East.

Paced by Elgin Baylor's 38.3 points a game, the Lakers were the best in the West at 54–26. Cincinnati improved to 43 wins as its second-year star Oscar Robertson averaged 30.8 points, 12.5 rebounds (amazing for a point guard), and 11.4 assists. No NBA player has averaged double figures in the three major categories before or since. Some experts began calling the Big O, not the Big Dipper, basketball's most complete player.

When the playoffs began, national focus returned to Boston. In the 1962 Eastern Division Finals, the giants clashed. Besides Wilt Chamberlain, the Warriors featured flashy passer Guy Rodgers, accurate shooter Paul Arizin, and ballhawk defender Al Attles. Boston had a more balanced lineup. Sharman had retired, but Tommy Heinsohn led them in scoring (22.3), Frank Ramsey in free-throw percentage (82.5), Bob Cousy in assists (7.8), Sam Jones in shooting accuracy (45.9), and Bill Russell in rebounds (24.9, a team record). Amazingly, none of those numbers outshone Chamberlain's season marks.

The Warriors and Celtics split the first six games, the home team

*Oscar Robertson shows off his passing skills. In the 1961–62
season, the 6'5" guard amazingly averaged a triple double—30.8 points,
12.5 rebounds, and 11.4 assists per game*

winning each contest. In game seven, Chamberlain blocked a shot in the waning seconds that was ruled goaltending. It gave Boston a 109–107 advantage. The Warriors tried a long pass off the backboard for Wilt at the buzzer, but as with the Hawks and Pettit in 1957, the tactic failed.

Boston advanced to the NBA finals to face a well-rested Lakers team that had quickly eliminated the Pistons. Los Angeles had no center nearly as talented as Russell, but they had the high-scoring combination of Elgin Baylor and guard Jerry West (30.8 ppg). Although only 6'5", Baylor averaged almost 19 rebounds a contest. The tight series went to a seventh game in Boston. The teams were tied with a few ticks of the clock remaining. Lakers guard Frank Selvy, who had scored 100 in a college game, shot from eight feet away. His attempt bounced off both sides of the rim and out. The Celtics rallied in overtime for the 110–107 win that secured a sixth championship trophy for William Felton Russell.

The ABL

The Celtics royalty and Chamberlain's numbers turned off many sports fans. Going into the 1962 season, the NBA had no national television contracts. Despite the presence of such young stars as Jerry West, Oscar Robertson, and Elgin Baylor, the NBA still added up to two inevitabilities: Wilt would score, and Boston would win. People called the Celtics the New York Yankees of the NBA. Their success took the suspense out of pro basketball. Because of this, Globetrotters entrepreneur Abe Saperstein organized a new league called the American Basketball League (ABL). The ABL placed franchises in three NBA cities: Chicago, San Francisco, and Los Angeles.

Although the ABL only lasted a season and a half, it had a major impact on basketball history for three important reasons. First, it admitted a black player named Connie Hawkins, a 6'8" New York City

John McLendon (right), coach of the short-lived ABL's Cleveland Pipers, welcomes Dick Barnett to the team in 1961. McLendon was the first black coach in professional basketball.

school-yard legend who was barred from the Big Ten and the NBA because of his rumored connection to a point-shaving scandal. Hawkins had never thrown a college game, but no college or NBA team would touch him. The ABL's Pittsburgh Rens gave Connie a chance.

Second, the owner of the ABL's Cleveland Pipers, a young businessman named George Steinbrenner, hired John McLendon, a black coach. McLendon had coached Tennessee State to three straight NCAA Division II titles and had turned out a few pro players. He was pro basketball's first black coach. The third significant contribution of the short-lived ABL was the introduction of a 25-foot arc beyond which all shots made counted for 3 points. That innovation later resurfaced in another pro league, the American Basketball Association (ABA), and was finally adopted in 1979 by the NBA.

Saperstein had formed the rival ABL in part to strike back at the NBA. The NBA's growth had ended the Globetrotters' monopoly on the nation's best black players. Although the Trotters were still popular on their world tours, they no longer had access to some of the NBA arenas where they had once been the main gate attraction.

A Respected Opponent

Bill Russell said that he enjoyed playing against Oscar Robertson more than any other opponent. Unlike most of the league's guards, the muscular 6'5", 210-pound Robertson challenged Russell, driving into the lane, head faking, and using his powerful hips and shoulders to shield the ball from defenders.

The Streak Continues

In the 1962–63 season, Cincinnati became a member of the NBA East. It was no blessing, as it put the Royals in the division owned by Boston. The Warriors moved from Philadelphia to San Francisco, where Wilt played in a 14,000-seat auditorium called the Cow Palace. The Lakers, however, won the realigned West over the Warriors, and the Celtics took the East by 10 games.

Bob Cousy—a Celtics living legend—announced that the season would be his last. For the first time Sam Jones led Boston in scoring with a 19.7 average, and Bill Russell pulled down 23.6 caroms a game for Boston. In the Eastern playoffs, it took Boston seven games to eliminate Cincinnati, and they won the NBA finals over Los Angeles 4–2.

At the beginning of the 1963–64 season, fans wondered how good the Celtics would be without Bob Cousy directing its fast breaks. Averaging 24.7 rebounds a game and leading Boston in minutes for the seventh straight time, Bill Russell dispelled the notion that the Celtics were Cousy's team. Though NBA fans did not know it, Russell played the season under such stress that he had a nervous breakdown. He covered up his personal problems for the good of the team.

League scoring in 1963–64 dipped to 110 points per team per game as coaches tried to emulate Boston by stressing defense. Even Wilt Chamberlain focused more on defending the basket, and his average dropped to 36.9 points, almost 14 less than his 1962 figure. San Francisco, which had won only 31 games the previous season (with the Stilt averaging nearly 45 points), won 48 in 1964 to win the West. Boston won 59 games to edge out an improved 55–25 Cincinnati squad in the East.

Boston prevailed over Cincinnati 4–1 in the Eastern finals, and San Francisco slipped past St. Louis to set up another Russell-Chamberlain showdown. Although fans concentrated on the matchup of the big men, the series was not close. In game five at the Garden, the Celtics captured their sixth straight league crown. Boston had held

Founding Father

On September 7, 1964, Celtics owner and NBA cofounder Walter Brown died. The man who had drafted Chuck Cooper, the NBA's first black draft choice and the Celtics' first black player, was remembered by the Boston players, who wore black bands across the shoulder of their singlets to commemorate him.

the Warriors under 100 points in three of the five games. Wilt did top Bill in one competition: Chamberlain's 1964 MVP award broke Russell's three-year MVP string.

Race Becomes an Issue

The 1964–65 season began with Chamberlain suffering pancreatitis and Elgin Baylor with bad knees. Red Auerbach sometimes started five black players: Sam and K. C. Jones, Willie Naulls, Thomas "Satch" Sanders, and Bill Russell. Sanders was a 6'6" defensive specialist out of NYU, and Naulls was Russell's old college rival at UCLA. Auerbach didn't even notice that he had put an all-black team on the court. He was focused on the players' skills, not their complexion. Sanders, Sam Jones, K. C. Jones, Naulls, and Russell were intelligent players and great defenders. They had played for strong collegiate programs and were good citizens. Nevertheless, fans noticed their color. A few NBA teams still had racial quotas in 1965, and the unwritten rule outside Boston was as follows: Start a maximum of three blacks and maintain a half-white roster. The overall balance in the league, however, had tipped. The NBA was now 55 percent black.

The early 1960s were a period of unprecedented racial tension in the United States. Medgar Evers, the Mississippi field secretary of the NAACP and a veteran of two foreign wars, was gunned down in his driveway on June 12, 1963. Boston's most recognizable black athletes, Bill Russell and Red Sox pitcher Earl Wilson, marched at Evers's funeral. The Evers assassination prompted President John F. Kennedy to deliver a national television address on the importance of racial equality, in which he quoted the economic gaps between white and black Americans.

On August 28, 1963, Dr. Martin Luther King Jr. delivered the keynote address to a crowd of 250,000 at the March on Washington. He spoke of his dream of black and white children playing together in the Deep South. Two weeks later, four young black girls in a Sunday school class at a Birmingham, Alabama, church died when the local Ku Klux Klan bombed their church building. In November, Kennedy fell victim to an assassin's bullet in Dallas. Many blacks felt that they had lost a strong ally in the struggle for justice. They recalled Kennedy helping free King from a Georgia prison in 1960 and his compassionate address on race after Evers's death. Some black Americans were wary of Kennedy's successor, Lyndon B. Johnson, who was a southerner.

The racial climate of the times became more volatile in 1964. Just 35-years-old, King won the Nobel Peace Prize that year, the youngest winner ever, but three civil rights workers—two young Jewish men and a young black man—were found dead in an earthen dam near Philadelphia, Mississippi, after being missing for two months. A policeman's fatal shooting of a black teenager led to a four-day riot in Harlem. Black Muslim leader Malcolm X predicted bloodier riots for U.S. cities. After upsetting Sonny Liston for the heavyweight crown, Cassius Clay announced that he was a Black Muslim who preferred to be called Cassius X.

Amid this turmoil, Auerbach put five black players on the basketball court. At the time, St. Louis was the sole NBA franchise in the south, and it had three black stars: playmaker Lenny Wilkens, bruising rebounder Bill Bridges, and 6'10" center Zelmo Beatty. League veterans felt the Hawks had cut other talented black players, such as small-college All-Americans Charlie Hardnett and Cleo Hill, to keep a player ratio that would not offend white season-ticket holders. Though Oscar Robertson was Cincinnati's leader, the Royals released such black players as Bob McCullough (a national scoring leader in college) and Rossie Johnson (on three Division II championship teams) in training camp. Many Royals fans drove up from neighboring Kentucky to attend games. The NBA had no black coaches or assistant coaches in 1965. Yet the league All-Star first team—Elgin Baylor, Jerry Lucas, Oscar Robertson, Jerry West, and Bill Russell—included three blacks, and the All-Star second team—Bob Pettit, Gus Johnson, Wilt Chamberlain, Sam Jones, and Hal Greer—featured four.

The Rivalry Continues

Boston finished the 1964–65 season at 62–18. Auerbach considers it his best team ever. Sam Jones set a Boston record by averaging 25.9 points. Wilt Chamberlain had been traded to the Philadelphia 76ers for three players. Even with Wilt, Philly went 40–40, ending up 22 games behind Boston. The Celtics and the Sixers met in the Eastern final. They split the first six games, sending the series back to Boston Garden for the deciding game.

Boston seemed to have the contest in hand, leading by four in the closing moments, when Chamberlain began to assert himself. Wilt scored a basket and was fouled. A notoriously poor free throw shooter (54 percent for his career), he converted the charity shot to bring the Sixers within a point. Behind 110–109, the Sixers tried to get the ball inside to the Big Dipper for a shot, but a turnover gave possession back to Boston. Now all the Celtics had to do was inbound the ball and kill the remaining two seconds, which separated Boston from a chance for a seventh straight league championship. Auerbach chose his tallest player, Russell, to inbound the ball. Attempting a lob pass, Russell threw the ball right into the guy wire that supported the backboard. Sixers ball. Perhaps this was an opportunity for Wilt's redemption. Time-out, Philadelphia.

As twenty million television viewers watched, Boston mapped out their final defense. Auerbach thought Chamberlain would be used as a decoy, with Hal Greer taking the last shot. Greer was Philly's best outside shooter. The Sixers surprised the Celtics by stationing the 6'3" Greer to inbound the ball. He aimed the pass at Chet "the Jet" Walker, a 6'7" forward, who was tall enough to lob the ball to Chamberlain. Out of nowhere, Boston's long-armed sixth man, John Havlicek, flashed to deflect the ball to teammate Sam Jones. In the most famous announcer's call in NBA history, gravel-voiced Celtic radio commentator Johnny Most yelled, "Havlicek steals it! Havlicek stole the ball. Havlicek stole the ball!" Sam Jones dribbled out the clock, chased by frantic 76ers. Celtics fans swarmed the court, lifting the stunned Havlicek onto their shoulders. The Celtics were Eastern champs again.

The finals were anticlimactic. Without Elgin Baylor, who missed the series with an injury, Jerry West averaged 40 points a game, but his teammates were not up to the task as the Lakers fell to the Celtics in five games. Seven consecutive pennants had been raised to the ceiling of Boston Garden. Boston had survived some close calls, but the four-leaf clovers on their warm-ups had seen them through.

Racial unrest reached a peak on August 11, 1965, when rumors of a police brutality case involving a black teen touched off six days of rioting in the Watts section of Los Angeles. Thirty-four people were killed in the violence, making it the bloodiest race riot in U.S. history.

Sparked by the matchup of their big men, the Celtics and the 76ers had become bitter Eastern rivals by the 1965–66 season. On January 1, 1966, Boston stood at 25–9, Philadelphia 21–13. On February 12, Boston took an 85–83 tug-of-war from the Sixers to grab a five-game lead in the East, but in early March, Philly swept a home-and-home series with Boston. They beat Boston six of ten times over the season and won the division by one game, with a 55–25 record.

NBA fans sensed a power shift. Wilt won his seventh straight

Big Bucks

In 1965, Bill Russell signed a contract paying him $100,001 a year. His logic was that he should be paid at least a dollar more than Wilt Chamberlain, whom he had bested in the Eastern Finals. Russell also pointed to his five MVP trophies, compared to Wilt's two. For the first time, by 1965 basketball players were earning more than football and baseball players.

scoring crown; he had led the league in every season that he had played in the NBA. He shot less now, and his average was 33.5. Other 76ers, such as Hal Greer and Chet Walker, contributed. Boston's reign seemed unsteady, and Wilt was obviously hungry for a championship. He was tired of magazine columns criticizing his selfish play and fed up with people praising Russell as a team player and a better defender. Underscoring his desire for a ring, the 1966 Philadelphia assist leader wasn't a guard; it was Wilt Chamberlain.

Boston played Cincinnati in the Eastern semis and won a tough five-game series that went the distance. By virtue of receiving a first-round bye, the 76ers were rested. The thought of Boston on the ropes against Cincinnati encouraged Philly's players and fans. Having won 18 of their last 21 games and armed with Wilt's new team-oriented attitude, Philly was confident that they could topple the Beantown squad. The days off, however, had actually robbed the Sixers of their competitive fire. Boston took the first two games convincingly. Philly took the third at home. Boston won game four in overtime and clinched the series in Philadelphia.

After Boston lost game one of the NBA Finals to the Lakers, Red Auerbach made public something that he had decided a week earlier: Bill Russell would coach the 1966–67 Celtics. Auerbach's announcement constituted the first time a black coach had been named to guide a major pro sports team. (Most sports historians don't consider the ABL, in which John McClendon coached the Cleveland franchise, a major league.) The psychological effect of the announcement was considerable. The Celtics were now playing to win one more championship for Red Auerbach. Sanders, Sam Jones, K. C. Jones, and Woody Sauldsberry anticipated playing for a black coach the next year. Boston won the next three games easily and won the game-seven clincher 95–93 at home. Exuberant players pushed Auerbach into the showers and doused him with champagne. Auerbach had guided the Celtics to nine NBA crowns in ten years, including eight straight.

End of an Era

As Bill Russell began his career as player-coach in the 1966–67 season, the NBA was two-thirds black. K. C. Jones had decided to retire, but Russell coaxed his friend into playing for him. Boston's nucleus of players were old by basketball standards: K. C. Jones was 35, Sam Jones was 34, and Russell would be 33 by season's end. Bailey Howell and Wayne Embry, who were acquired to help Russell on the glass, were both 30 years old. The only young key player was John Havlicek.

In Philadelphia, coach Alex Hannum surrounded Wilt Chamberlain with a strong young supporting cast: veteran guards Hal Greer, Wally Jones, and Larry Costello; small forward Chet Walker; and power forward Lucius Jackson, who helped Wilt defend the lane. Off the bench, 6'7" leaper Billy "Kangaroo Kid" Cunningham was a sixth man equal to Havlicek. Now Chamberlain was truly able to focus on defense and rebounding. In the first Boston-Philly meeting with Russell as player-coach, Boston bowed 138–96. In their first 31 games, the 76ers reeled off 28 wins, a league record. Philly had a 45–4 record at one point, the best run in the history of professional sport.

Although Boston won five of nine games against Philly, the Sixers finished with a league record 68–13, eight games in front of Boston. Sacrificing scoring for the defensive boards, Wilt averaged only 24.1 points, but he placed third in the league in assists. Wilt made 68.3 percent of his shots, a tribute to his shot selection.

In Russell's first playoff as a coach, Boston beat a feisty young New York team 3 games to 1. Philly beat Cincinnati by the same margin. In the Eastern Finals, the Sixers won the first three games, with Chamberlain grabbing 41 rebounds in game three, a playoff record. Game four was played April 9, 1967, on national television. Fans tuned in Sunday afternoon to witness the unthinkable—a possible sweep of the Celtics, but Sam Jones scored 32 and Havlicek 31 to give Boston a four-point victory.

In game five, Boston led after the first quarter 37-26. Russell had 10 rebounds to Chamberlain's 5. Russell appeared to have his club back in the hunt, but Chamberlain turned things around with his shooting, rebounding, and shot blocking. Philly put together a 22–9 run to lead at halftime 70-65. The third period belonged to former Villanova star Wally Jones, who hit eight of nine shots. Rebounding proved to be the Celtics weakness. Chamberlain, Lucius Jackson, and Billy Cunningham overmatched Russell on the glass, and the final period began with Philly up by six. The Sixers went on a rampage, running up a 27-point lead en route to a 140-116 victory. The Celtics juggernaut had finally run aground, a victim of the team's age and style of play. Boston would not participate in the finals for the first time in a decade—since Russell had joined the organization. In a very high-scoring series, Philly triumphed over Wilt's old San Francisco Warriors in six games.

During the summer of 1967, everywhere Russell went in Massachusetts, fans asked him what had happened to the mighty Celtics. As if winning were easy. As if nine straight titles weren't sufficient. As if Wilt Chamberlain and a cast of stars were a pushover. As if playing and coaching was not a challenge. The Celtics were older and slower. They had done well to win 60 games the previous year. Boston fans were spoiled.

A Wider World

America experienced another long hot summer of racial disturbance in 1967. Newark police reported more than 30 dead after several nights of rioting provoked by police arrest of a cabdriver. In Detroit, a police raid of an after-hours bar in August incensed inner-city blacks, and a week of looting, sniper fire, and arson resulted in 43 deaths.

Things other than basketball concerned Bill Russell. He had two sons. He was an avid golfer. A few years earlier, he had told his father he made enough money for his dad not to have to pour molten iron for a living. Bill made cameo appearances on a new television series, *Cowboy in Africa*, starring former Celtics backup and *Rifleman* star Chuck Connors.

America's racial situation still bothered Russell. When Bill drove to Louisiana to visit his retired father, his sons would complain of hunger. Although he was a world-famous athlete and carried about $2,000 in his wallet, no Southern restaurant would serve his family a meal.

Russell had helped take basketball around the world. His Olympic squad toured Latin America, giving clinics and playing exhibitions along the way. When Russell was an NBA veteran, the State Department organized a goodwill basketball tour of Latin America. Because Russell had been to Latin America on the game's behalf already, he asked that an African tour be arranged. In countries such as Ethiopia and Egypt, Russell taught the fundamentals of basketball to groups of poor children. The poverty he saw in his travels and the prejudice he experienced at home put the game of basketball and his success in perspective.

In the 1967–68 season, Russell coached Boston to a second-place finish behind Philadelphia in the East. In the playoffs, the Celtics trailed Detroit 2–1 before recovering for a 4–2 series win, and the Sixers won their series against the Knicks but lost Billy Cunningham to a broken wrist. The teams were scheduled to begin the Eastern Finals on April 5, 1968. The day before the first game, Martin Luther King Jr. was assassinated. The teams decided to play the opener, but the mood was somber as Boston won 127-118. The series was suspended until after the King funeral, a nationally televised event attended by Wilt Chamberlain. When the series resumed, Philly won three straight. Boston appeared to be on the verge of early elimination for the second consecutive season. People were saying Russell was doing too much by playing and coaching. Auerbach was the secret, critics wrote. Boston bounced back, taking the final three games and earn-

Changing of the Guard

Following Bill Russell's 1969 retirement, a new star, 7'1" Lew Alcindor, entered the NBA. A three-time NCAA champion at UCLA, Alcindor changed his name to Kareem Abdul-Jabbar in 1971. Abdul-Jabbar would go on to break Wilt Chamberlain's seemingly insurmountable career scoring record, amassing 38,387 points and winning six MVP awards in his 20-year career. Although he did not equal Russell's record 11 NBA titles, Abdul-Jabbar did play on six championship teams.

ing a berth in the finals against Los Angeles. The Celtics won the series in six games, giving Russell his tenth NBA title and his first as a coach.

All of the 1968–69 key Celtics players, except for 28-year-old John Havlicek, were over 30. In the season opener, Russell sent the league a message with a 36-rebound performance against the Pistons. Young teams were establishing themselves as threats to the Celtics. Baltimore won the East with its new stars Wes Unseld and Earl "the Pearl" Monroe. Unseld, who had been the first black player at the University of Louisville, was voted Rookie of the Year and MVP in 1969.

Russell's team turned it on in the playoffs. Without the home-court advantage because of their fourth-place finish, the Celtics defeated the Sixers in five games and the emerging Knicks, who starred Willis Reed and Walt Frazier, in six games.

These victories set up the final Russell-Chamberlain showdown. The Sixers had traded Chamberlain to Los Angeles. Lakers owner Jack Kent Cooke was building a new arena, the Forum, and he wanted the Elgin Baylor–Jerry West–Wilt Chamberlain trio to start a championship tradition. Russell had announced that he was going to retire at the end of the season, and the Celtics were motivated to send him out as a winner. The flashy, gold-clad Angelenos had other ideas.

Jerry "Mr. Clutch" West lit up the scoreboard for 53 points, leading the Lakers to a 120-118 victory in game one. West was still smoking in game two, as his 41 points keyed another Lakers win. The Celtics knotted the series at 2–2, but the Lakers took game five behind West's 39 points. West pulled a hamstring muscle in his leg, which slowed him in game six. The heavily bandaged guard managed 26 points, but Boston won and tied the series at three games apiece.

Now Russell was on the brink of something that even Red Auerbach had never achieved—coaching a team to an NBA championship from a 2–0 deficit. His inspired teammates had given him a 100–83 cushion with nine minutes to go when Mr. Clutch came alive. The injured West scored 14 of the Lakers next 19 points. He didn't get much help from the aging Baylor or from Chamberlain, whom Russell nullified. Wilt sat out the closing moments with a sore knee, a decision Russell later criticized in the postgame press conference. A warrior, taught Russell, goes out on his feet. Despite West's courageous effort—42 points, 13 rebounds, 12 assists—Boston captured an eleventh NBA championship with a 108–106 victory. Bill Russell had played on eleven champions in thirteen seasons. Along with Sam Jones, Bill Russell retired after the 1969 NBA Finals. The following season, Boston had a losing record.

In 1974, Bill Russell learned that he had been voted into the Basketball Hall of Fame. Russell had said years earlier that he would not attend induction ceremonies if elected, and he kept his word. He never believed in signing autographs, which he called worthless, and award ceremonies, which he called redundant. Russell went on to coach and serve as general manager of both the Seattle Supersonics and the Sacramento Kings and to work as an NBA television commentator. He remains the league's number two all-time rebounder.

CHAPTER 4

The Big Dipper

Wilt Chamberlain is arguably the most dominant modern athlete ever to rule a team sport. Even in light of Michael Jordan's accomplishments, Wilt's feats are astounding. They include

- 100 points in an NBA game
- a 50.4-point single-season scoring average in 1961-62 (Jordan's highest, 37.1)
- a 33-game winning streak with the 1972-73 Los Angeles Lakers
- a 55-rebound game against Bill Russell and the Boston Celtics
- a streak of 35 baskets made without a miss
- 1,045 games played without fouling out.

Chamberlain dunked so easily over defenders he earned the nickname the Big Dipper. Despite his immense talent, he was one of the most unpopular basketball players of all time. Fans saw him as a villain, not a hero.

Wilton Norman Chamberlain was born in Philadelphia on August 21, 1936. He was unusually long at birth—more than 29 inches. At age 9, a bout with pneumonia almost killed him, and he missed a year of school. At age 12, when he stood 6'2", he and a friend started a painting company. Wilt dreamed of being an Olympic track star. That year, 1948, high jumper Alice Coachman became the first black woman to win an Olympic gold medal. Coachman had been a college basketball star.

As a boy Wilt Chamberlain once grew four inches in seven weeks. At 15, Wilt stood 6'11". He played basketball in the Police Athletic League and led his YMCA team to a national championship. He enrolled at Overbrook High School, where he earned All-City honors three times, scoring 92 points in one game, and was the most heavily recruited schoolboy basketball player in history. In tenth grade he went on his first college recruiting visit—to Dayton University. The NBA's Philadelphia Warriors even secured his territorial draft rights while Wilt was a high schooler. Seventy-seven major and 128 smaller colleges wrote to Chamberlain, and on May 14, 1955, he decided to go to the University of Kansas. When Wilt chose Kansas over several Philadelphia colleges with strong basketball traditions, the NCAA, FBI, and Internal Revenue Service opened investigations to see whether he was being illegally paid.

Big Man on Campus

At Kansas, 14,000 fans attended Wilt's freshman basketball debut, a school attendance record at a university where basketball inventor Dr. James Naismith had coached and the game had been played since 1899. The freshman squad beat the varsity as Wilt poured in 42 points and grabbed 29 rebounds despite a triple-teaming defense. Under NCAA rules, freshmen could not play varsity sports, so Wilt spent his first season at Kansas on the freshman team.

In preparation for the 1956–57 season, basketball players at Northwestern University saw an action photo of Wilt in a game with his

The Jayhawks' Wilt Chamberlain snatches a rebound against archrival Kansas State. Chamberlain became weary of the college game because of the fouling and other dirty tactics used by opposing teams to slow down his scoring. He left college after his junior year to join the Globetrotters.

elbows above the rim and assumed the picture was a result of trick photography. The visiting team was sure that Wilt was standing on a stool in the photo. When the teams met, the Wildcats saw Wilt leap and believed their eyes. Kansas beat Northwestern 87-69, as Wilt sank 20 baskets in 29 attempts for 52 points and 31 rebounds, both school records. In a 78-61 romp over Marquette, Wilt scored 39, snared 22 boards, and rejected 14 shots. The Jayhawks went undefeated in 12 contests before losing to Iowa State by a basket. They won five more in a row by almost 20 points a game. In the 1956–57 season, Kansas went 21–2, the school's best record in 20 years. They won the Big Eight Conference title and received a bid to the NCAA tournament. The Jayhawks were scheduled to play their first-round game in Dallas, but the team stayed in a hotel in Grand Prairie, Texas. Chamberlain thought it was a measure by the coaches to keep the team away from the limelight. It was actually because no Dallas hotels would admit black players.

In the regional opener Kansas faced Southern Methodist University and 6'8" All-Southwest center Jim Krebs. SMU had won 36 straight in their fieldhouse. Wilt outpointed Krebs 36–22, and Kansas won, 73-65. (Krebs went on to play seven seasons for the NBA Lakers.) In round two, Oklahoma City players tried to anger Wilt with racial taunts. They poked him and tripped him. Kansas won, 81–61, and one Oklahoma City player, Hubert "Hub" Reed, apologized to Wilt for his teammates' behavior.

In the national semifinals, Kansas used 8-0 and 16-0 runs to topple the University of San Francisco 80-56. In the other semifinal, North Carolina edged Michigan in triple overtime. That pitted No. 1 North Carolina (31–0) against No. 2 Kansas (24–2). The Tar Heels tried to psyche out Wilt on the opening tip-off. They deployed a 5'11" player for the jump ball against Chamberlain. The maneuver seemed to confuse the Jayhawks, who fell behind 9-2 and then 19-7 as the Tar Heels made their first nine shots. By halftime, Kansas was shooting only 27.3 percent to Carolina's 64.5. North Carolina held the ball after intermission, but Kansas moved ahead 40-37. The Heels worked it to a tie, sending the game into an extra period. Two overtime periods later, North Carolina won the NCAA title by a point. Wilt had averaged 30 points, 19 rebounds, and 9 blocked shots as a sophomore.

Wilt won the Big Eight indoor high jump championship in 1957. He cleared the bar at a height of 6'8". He also won the 440-yard dash in the Kansas Relays. Wilt was so strong that he routinely beat Kansas shot putters and discus throwers Bill Neider and Al Oerter in arm wrestling. In footraces he could beat anyone on campus except All-American miler Wes Santee.

Despite the loss of three starters from the NCAA Finals team, the 1957–58 Jayhawks won their first four games. In Wilt's only college performance in his hometown, KU beat St. Joseph's in Philadelphia, 66-54. Wilt contributed 31 points—as usual, close to half of Kansas's production.

In the Big Eight opener, Kansas downed rival Kansas State 79-65. KU won ten straight and were ranked No. 1 nationally. In another victory over Kansas State, Wilt was accidentally kneed in the groin. He had to sit out two games, both of which the Jayhawks lost by a basket. Chamberlain returned against Colorado, scoring 32 of his team's 67 points in a 21-point pasting of the Buffaloes. In the next game, against Missouri, Wilt pumped in 35 for a 68-54 win. He fouled out of that game, but the Big Dipper would never foul out of another college or professional competition again—a record that will likely never be broken.

In the Big Eight championship, Kansas bowed to Kansas State in overtime, 79-75. Although Kansas had won two of three games against K State, the Wildcats owned the better conference record and received that NCAA tournament bid. (At that time, only 16 teams made it to the NCAAs, and only one team from a conference received a bid.)

The Thrill Is Gone

Four NCAA rule changes were instituted during Wilt's brief college career. The inbounds pass over the backboard was outlawed because

KU often lobbed the ball over the backboard to Wilt, who would dunk it. The new rule required that an inbound pass must travel under or alongside the backboard. Players were also prohibited from guiding in a teammate's shot above the rim. It was also ruled that during a free throw the non-shooting team had to have two of its players on either side of the lane closest to the basket. And players were prohibited from breaking an imaginary plane at the foul line until their own free throw touched the rim. The last rule was to prevent Wilt from taking off after releasing a free throw and leaping to tap in his own missed shot.

Vickers Petroleum offered Wilt a job selling tires so he could play on their AAU basketball squad. (This practice is prohibited under current NCAA rules.) Wilt enjoyed basketball on the AAU level, and he had fun playing in school yards and at Kutscher's Country Club in upstate New York, where Red Auerbach was his coach. It was the college game that he disliked. Other teams froze the ball against Kansas or shoved Chamberlain around. In one game, Oklahoma State passed 160 times before taking a shot. Teams, including perennial power Kentucky, removed Kansas from their schedule. By this point, Wilt had stopped attending classes and had lost all interest in school.

Wilt knew former Globetrotters star Goose Tatum, whom he often saw in Kansas City. Tatum was starting his own team and offered Wilt $100,000 to join it. Philadelphia Warriors owner Eddie Gottlieb, who owned territorial draft rights to Wilt, asked for NBA owners' approval to sign Wilt after his sophomore season. Gottlieb was voted down; no player could be drafted until his class graduated. At Toots Shors' restaurant in New York City, Chamberlain announced that he was passing up his senior year at Kansas and signing with the Globetrotters for a reported $65,000 (really $46,000 with bonuses). The time spent with the Globetrotters matured Wilt. The 19-year-old could finally play basketball for fun, without being triple-teamed or pounded around. He saw the world, traveling to Italy, France, Austria, and Germany. He toured with older men who gave him pointers about foreign food, languages, and enjoying life. On the court, the Trotter routines improved his ballhandling and passing.

The Game's Most Dominant Player

After a year with the Globetrotters, Wilt was ready for the NBA, but the league was not ready for him. His first-year salary with the Warriors was $65,000, double what Boston All-Star Bob Cousy was earning. In 1959–60, Wilt averaged 37.6 points as a rookie, and he scored 50 points in a game seven times. He was named Rookie of the Year and the league's Most Valuable Player. In his second campaign, Chamberlain averaged 38.4 points a game, including a 78-point barrage against Elgin Baylor's Lakers. In 1961–62 he had a 50.4 scoring average, becoming the first (and only) player to score 4,000 points in an NBA season; no NBA player had scored even 2,000 in a season until 1958.

Opposing fans began to boo Wilt, thinking that the game came too easy for him. He could score effortlessly and his height gave him an unfair advantage, they argued. Using Boston's Bill Russell as an example, sportswriters criticized him for not bringing a championship to the University of Kansas or Philadelphia. They pointed out that Russell was an unselfish player, unconcerned with personal statistics, and his team had won NBA titles. What the sportswriters wrote was true, but their remarks hurt Chamberlain. No one understood him. "Nobody roots for Goliath," he observed.

Despite his lack of popularity, Wilt still enjoyed the life of a celebrity. He bought racehorses, dated actresses, and drove an expensive Bentley automobile. Instantly recognizable in a crowd, he was a hero to black children—a larger-than-life superman. New York fans flocked to his summer league games in Harlem's outdoor Rucker Tournament. A 7' New York high school player, Lew Alcindor, met Chamberlain there. Alcindor began to walk, dress, and comb his hair like the Big Dipper.

In the 1961–62 season, Wilt had notched two 59-point games and

UCLA's Lew Alcindor (Kareem Abdul-Jabbar) takes off for a jam. The NCAA outlawed the dunk after Alcindor's first collegiate season (1966–67).

a 67-point game against the hapless New York Knicks. The two Eastern rivals met again on March 2, 1962, in a small arena in Hershey, Pennsylvania, a city famous for manufacturing chocolate. Only 4,124 fans attended. The Knicks always double-teamed Chamberlain with two young 6'11" players: Cleveland Buckner, who had been All-Conference at Jackson State, and former California All-American and 1960 Olympian Darrel Imhoff. Nothing worked. The Knicks coach ordered his big men to foul Wilt, whose only weakness was free-throw shooting. He usually made only about half his shots from the charity stripe.

Wilt scored on a dizzying array of fall-away bank shots, finger rolls, and slams for 23 first-quarter points. He had 41 by halftime. Warriors coach Frank McGuire could either rest his star center or ask him to pour it on. Angry because of the Knicks' fouling tactics, McGuire chose the latter.

Little Big Man

Guy Rodgers never received the attention of Bob Cousy or Oscar Robertson, but he tied Cousy's league mark of 28 assists in one game. Rodgers, a 6'0", 180-pound former All-American at Temple, combined Cousy's flair with Robertson's keen sense of the game. He averaged 18 points for San Francisco in both 1963-64 and 1964-65. He gathered 509 rebounds in 1961, good numbers for a playmaker. Rodgers played in four NBA All-Star games, where he delighted fans with his brilliant look-away passes. It was Guy Rodgers who set Chamberlain up for all those dunks, fall-away jumpers, and finger rolls. Rodgers retired with 6,917 assists, 286 more feeds in 46 playoff games (for a 6.2 average), and a one-game assist record that stood for 15 years. He was the first black playmaker in the NBA with pizzazz.

Early in the fourth quarter, the unstoppable Dipper broke his own NBA scoring mark with his 79th point. Maybe Philly would take him out of the game now. No chance. The Hershey fans, who had braved the cold to see a rare Warriors game there, began to chant, "A hundred! A hundred!"

Wilt Chamberlain's 100-point Game

Here are the Big Dipper's record-setting statistics by period:

	Min.	FGM	FGA	FTM	FTA	REB	A	Pts
1	12	7	14	9	9	10	0	23
2	12	7	12	4	5	4	1	18
3	12	10	16	8	8	6	1	28
4	12	12	21	7	10	5	0	31
Totals	48	36	63	28	32	25	2	100

Chamberlain could hear them in the small arena, and he thought, "A hundred? They're crazy!" But he knew that he had scored 92 in a 32-minute high school game, and the Warriors kept feeding him the ball. Good players, such as Paul Arizin and Guy Rodgers, passed up open shots to set up their teammate. With 42 seconds left in the clock, Wilt dunked home his 100th point. Fans streamed onto the court and surrounded Chamberlain, congratulating him. The court was cleared so that the clock could run down. Philadelphia had won 169–147. Wilt had scored 59 points in the second half. The most telling line in the game's box score was Chamberlain's free-throw statistics: He had made 28 of 32 foul shots.

The Warriors moved to San Francisco for the 1962–63 season. Wilt continued to dominate the league, producing 73- and 72-point games in November. He was hungry for an NBA title to silence his critics. Wilt's 1962–63 scoring average of 44.8 is still the second best in history. Despite Wilt's efforts, his Warriors lost a showdown in the 1964 playoffs with Russell and Boston 4–1, and Chamberlain was once again labeled a loser in the sports pages. Wilt's few supporters pointed out that Russell had a superior supporting cast.

Chamberlain was traded to the Philadelphia 76ers in 1964. The

Chamberlain shows how many points he scored against the Knicks on March 2, 1962. Along with his record-setting scoring performance, he also pulled down 25 rebounds and dished out 2 assists.

Warriors record plummeted from 48–32 in 1963–64 (with Wilt) to 17–63 in 1964–65 (without Wilt). Chamberlain kept putting up incredible stats, but the Sixers lost to Bill Russell's Celtics in the 1965 and 1966 playoffs. For the 1966–67 season, Sixers coach Alex Hannum instructed Wilt to concentrate on rebounding, defense, and passing when he was double- and triple-teamed. Hannum figured if two or more men were guarding Wilt, good scorers such as Chet Walker, Hal Greer, and Billy Cunningham could get open shots. Philadelphia jumped out to a 22–2 start and finished the season with 68 wins—an NBA record. The Sixers eliminated their nemesis, the Celtics, in

Rule Change

For the 1964-65 season, the NBA introduced a rule change to make Chamberlain, Russell, and other big men less effective. The free-throw lane was widened from 12 feet to 16 feet, which made it more difficult for post players to position themselves close to the basket. To avoid a three-second violation, players had to move in and out of the enlarged lane area.

the Eastern playoff finals and beat Wilt's former team, San Francisco, 4–2 in the league finals. At age 30, Wilt had finally shown the world he could play team basketball and win.

After the 1967–68 season, Chamberlain was traded to Los Angeles, where experts thought he, Elgin Baylor, and Jerry West would form a powerhouse squad. Baylor was injured most of the 1968–69 season, and the Lakers lost seven-game NBA finals in both 1969 (to Boston) and 1970 (to New York). Chamberlain won his second NBA title with the Lakers in 1972, beating New York 4–1.

Wilt had arrived at the twilight of his career. Bill Russell had retired, and Kareem Abdul-Jabbar was his chief rival. He had nothing else to prove: He had played all over the world and owned most of the significant NBA records. Although Wilt is largely remembered as a loser, his 1967 Sixers team and 1972 Lakers team (which won 33

Chamberlain dunks over Jerry Lucas during the 1972 NBA Finals. The Lakers won the series over the Knicks 4–1.

straight) posted the best won-loss records in NBA history up to that point. After playing 14 NBA seasons, Chamberlain retired following the 1972–73 season, after his Lakers team had lost to the Knicks in the NBA Finals.

An Amazing Career

It is difficult to imagine a performer such as Chamberlain in today's team-oriented NBA game. Wilt's big numbers and rare height filled seats. In 1961–62, he averaged 50.4 points and 25.7 rebounds, twice what is considered an outstanding average today. He played all but eight minutes that season, averaging an amazing 48.5 minutes a game (because Philly was involved in seven overtime contests). He led the NBA in minutes played each of his first seven seasons, an admirable feat for a man who was shoved around, grabbed, and surrounded every time he touched the ball. Rather than whine about the rough tactics used against him, Wilt displayed maturity and sportsmanship by excelling in spite of them.

When Chamberlain left the University of Kansas in 1958, a reporter from *Look* magazine interviewed the teenage seven-footer about his decision to leave college early. He explained to the reporter why the game was no fun. Opponents stalled with the basketball to keep it from Kansas and assigned two or three players against him in the low post. Teams resorted to tugging Chamberlain's shorts, stepping on his feet, and even tying invisible chicken wire above the KU basket to deflect his shots. Wilt's decision to forego his senior season is meaningful considering how much he loved to play. He had played in many leagues, including the Kutscher's Country Club League, the Police Athletic League, and YMCA leagues, and in the school yards of West Philly, which produced such NBA players as Jackie Moore, Wayne Hightower, Walt Hazzard, and Wali Jones. He played on New York playgrounds, in Chicago, in Indianapolis with Oscar Robertson, in Washington, D.C., and against John Thompson (now

Georgetown coach) and Elgin Baylor. Only against collegians was the game a thankless chore.

During the 1965–66 NBA season, *Sports Illustrated* ran a cover story with a title Wilt never approved: "My Life in a Bush League." Wilt did not call the NBA a minor league in the feature, but basketball was far less popular than pro football and baseball at the time. The league suffered from a number of problems. The Celtics dominated the league, taking the suspense out of the game. Most televised games were Sunday showdowns between Boston and Philadelphia. By 1966 the league was more than 60 percent black; the television audience was almost 80 percent white. Major-league baseball (1869) and pro football (1919) had started decades before the NBA (1949). When the *SI* cover story appeared, the league chastised Wilt for criticizing a few opponents, and he was fined because of the article's title.

Wilt was not a typical professional athlete. He bought a popular Harlem nightclub and renamed it Big Wilt's Small's Paradise. He worked there 18 hours a day in the off-season before turning over management to a friend. Between 1965 and 1968, Chamberlain commuted from New York to Philadelphia to play. He hobnobbed with authors, actresses, and jazz musicians, some of whom frequented his nightclub. Wilt, who had been the campus jazz and rock-and-roll deejay in college, cut a single, "By the River," which reached number 14 on the Boston charts. By his own admission his voice was nothing special.

The media had created the impression that Chamberlain and Bill Russell despised each other. In reality the basketball rivals were good friends during their playing days. They ate dinner at each other's homes on road trips. They dined out together. For five years, the Celtics and Sixers played a Thanksgiving game in Philadelphia, and Russell had a standing dinner invitation at Wilt's mother's house. For such competitors, the two centers were very civil and mutually respectful. Sportswriters built up the blood feud to promote games. It was good for the league.

Later in his career, Wilt became unpopular with black fans and black Americans in general. He never marched in civil rights demonstrations, and unlike Bill Russell, Elgin Baylor, and Oscar Robertson, he wasn't vocal when the NBA players fought for union rights. In 1968, Chamberlain met Republican presidential candidate Richard Nixon and decided he agreed with his policies. When Wilt announced his support of Nixon, magazines called him "The World's Tallest Nixon Supporter." Many black Americans were appalled. The Democratic party, under John Kennedy and Lyndon Johnson, had pushed through bills on civil rights, voting rights for blacks, and fair housing. Johnson had invited black leaders to the White House. The nation's three black mayors were Democrats.

Chamberlain's endorsement of a Republican made him appear out of step with the black community. Many wondered whether he had carefully researched his issues. Nixon, for instance, was running on a law-and-order platform, a phrase some blacks saw as a euphemism for increased police presence in the cities. Black youths were already mistrustful of insensitive police officers, who were mostly white and male, even in such cities as Atlanta, Detroit, and Washington, D.C., which were predominantly black. A few black leaders called Chamberlain an Uncle Tom, a label applied to blacks who behaved in deference to whites. Undeterred, Wilt attended the 1968 Republican Convention in Miami and stood by Nixon through the early years of his presidency. At a time when blacks looked up to defiant, proud athletes such as boxer Muhammad Ali, who refused induction into the army for the Vietnam War on religious grounds, Chamberlain certainly stood out. He even challenged Ali to a prizefight, though not because of their political differences. The bout, for which Wilt would have been paid $500,000, never came off.

Although many fans and sportswriters scorned him, Wilt helped transform the NBA into a major league and a profitable business. Today's NBA superstars can thank him for paving the way for their million-dollar contracts and product endorsements.

CHAPTER 5

The NBA's First High Flyer

Today, Michael Jordan, Charles Barkley, and Shawn Kemp soar through the air to score baskets with thunderous dunks. The phrase "above the rim" is often used to describe the attitude of today's NBA. Dunking is common, even by smaller players, such as Spud Webb and Robert Pack. High school and college players like to punctuate a fast break with a slam. A few women in college basketball have stuffed the ball home in competition.

In its first decade, the NBA boasted a few leapers, most notably Jumpin' Joe Fulks of Philadelphia, the league's first scoring leader, and George "Bird" Yardley, the first player to score 2,000 points in a season (1957–58). The 1950s style of play, however, featured a lot of set shots (flat-footed shots). Some teams ran fast breaks, but Fulks and Yardley used their elevation to rebound, shoot jumpers, and score close to the basket. Players did not take off from the foul lane, which was protected by tall centers and forwards, and sail to the goal. But in the 1958–59 season, rookie Elgin Baylor became the NBA's first true aerial act and revolutionized the way the game was played.

A Star Is Born

Elgin Gay Baylor was born in Washington, D.C., on September 16, 1934. He attended Spingarn High School. Baylor was the District's first black player named to the All-City team. Because Baylor hopped by defenders to score, sportswriters called the Spingarn team Rabbit Baylor and his Bunnies. They won a Division Two (black) city title.

Elgin went to the College of Idaho to play football and basketball. He averaged 31.3 points there in 1955 but then transferred to Seattle University. After sitting out a year, he averaged 29.7 points and 20 rebounds for Seattle in 1956–1957. Seattle coach John Castellani said Baylor possessed the grace of a gymnast and the accuracy of an adding machine. In the 1957–58 season, Elgin averaged 32.5 points and 19.3 rebounds and was named an All-American (along with Wilt Chamberlain and Oscar Robertson). Fans marveled at his ability to score off-balance and to twist inside defenders for spectacular baskets. The Seattle squad went 23–4 before losing to the more balanced Kentucky team in the NCAA finals. Baylor was named the tournament's Most Valuable Player.

On to the Pros

The Minneapolis Lakers had the first pick in the 1958 NBA draft, and they selected Baylor. The rookie took the league by storm. No player before had driven so strongly to the hoop, and Baylor's powerful upper body enabled him to pull up anywhere and score, even over centers. He swooped into the lane, palming the ball away from his body in one hand. He hung in the air on his hesitation jump shot, then released the ball after the defender touched down. He snared rebounds with his strong, sure hands. In one game during his rookie season, Baylor scored 55 points. He was co-MVP of his first All-Star Game.

By adding the eventual Rookie of the Year to its roster, the team improved its record by 14 games in the 1958–59 season. After defeating the Pistons in the Western semifinals, the Lakers upset the Hawks by taking three straight games after falling behind 2–1. The Hawks had finished 16 games ahead of the upstart Lakers in the regular season. In the NBA Finals, Red Auerbach's Celtics dynasty swept the young Lakers 4–0.

In the 1959–60 season, Baylor averaged 29.6 points and 16.4 rebounds. In only 32 minutes in the 1960 All-Star Game, Baylor scored 24 points and was named co-MVP with Bob Pettit. Despite finishing a dismal 25–50 in the regular season, the Lakers made it to the playoffs. They upset the Pistons in the Western semifinals and took the Hawks, who had a 46–29 regular-season record, to seven games before bowing out in the division finals.

When the Lakers moved to Los Angeles before the 1960–61 season, Tinseltown fans immediately took to the airborne player in the pretty gold-and-purple uniform. In school yards all over America, young players tried to imitate Baylor's drives, twists, and off-balance shots. But his All-Star status did not go to his head. He still played pickup games, often at Kelly Miller playground or Turkey Thicket playground in his native Washington, D.C. Only Baylor could score with his unorthodox release, and he hung in the air and put English, or spin, on his bank shots. He scored on second efforts by following his missed shots.

Baylor made headlines during the 1960–61 season. In a November game at Madison Square Garden, Baylor tallied 15 first quarter points, 19 in the second period, and 13 in the third for 47 points. Bored with their hapless Knicks, Garden fans started chanting, "give it to Elgin, Give it to Elgin!" The Lakers responded by going to Baylor, which made him uncomfortable. He was an unselfish player, priding himself not just on scoring but on rebounding and skillful passing as well. He added 24 fourth quarter points for a total of 71, which established a league record (broken the following season by Wilt

Elgin Baylor glides to the basket for 2 of his 42 points against the Royals on December 12, 1962. The NBA's first aerial artist, Baylor revolutionized the way in which basketball is played.

Chamberlain). In 1960–61, Elgin averaged 34.8 points a game and 19.8 rebounds. Elgin averaged 34 again in 1963. Against the perennial NBA champion Boston Celtics, he had 61 points in a playoff game— a record that stood until Jordan totaled 63 against the 1986 Celtics.

Boycott

Besides being a leader on the court, Elgin Baylor was also a spokesman for players' rights. At the 1964 All-Star Game, Baylor and Oscar Robertson led NBA players in a threatened boycott of the game over a demand for a larger pension fund for players. Lakers owner Bob Short ordered his two stars, Jerry West and Elgin Baylor, to play in the game or else. Short's ultimatum united the players. The game was played as scheduled when ABC, which was televising the game, stepped in and pressured the owners to concede to the players' demands.

Elgin's jovial attitude kept the Lakers loose. There was great pressure to win in Los Angeles because of all the celebrity fans and the presence of West and Baylor. Elgin played practical jokes on teammates, invented slang expressions, and was the central figure in Lakers card games. Opponents, including Bill Russell and Oscar Robertson, befriended Baylor.

Near the end of the 1964–65 season, Elgin Baylor shattered his knee. It was generally assumed to be a career-ending injury. His doctors set 99–1 odds against Baylor playing again; basketball is an explosive sport in which healthy knees are critical. Elgin exercised and rehabilitated his knee for five painful months. (With today's arthroscopic surgery, Baylor's recovery would have been faster.) He returned to action the next year, but his scoring average for the 1965–66 season was 16.6—half his usual production. He did manage a 28-point game and then a 46-point, 17-rebound effort against the Knicks. He was as explosive as ever; the only comparable leapers in the league were Knicks forward Jumpin' Johnny Green and Royals forward Tom Hawkins. Green and Hawkins were talented players but not 30-point scorers.

On October 28, 1966, against the Knicks, with two minutes left in the first half, Elgin dove for a loose ball and New York's Dick Van Arsdale landed on his knee. Elgin rolled away in obvious pain as the arena grew silent. The injury put Baylor in another leg cast. Again, the determined athlete recovered, showing his teammates how persistent he was. A healthier Baylor averaged 26.6 points and 12.8 rebounds a game in the 1966–67 season. Continuing his second comeback, Baylor averaged 26 points and grabbed 941 rebounds in the 1967–68 season, leading the Lakers to another NBA final. For the fifth time in the decade, the Lakers fell to the Celtics in the championship series. In 1968–69, the 34-year-old forward averaged 24.8 points while playing at about 75-percent effectiveness. Because his knees were fragile, Elgin relied on cunning and experience. The Lakers, despite adding Wilt Chamberlain to the team during the off-season, lost yet another final to Boston in 1969—their sixth with Baylor and West. This time it was a close seven-game series.

The Chamberlain-led Lakers did make the 1970 league finals. Baylor had averaged 24.0 points and 10.4 rebounds during the regular season. A jump-shooting, defense-oriented Knicks team beat Los Angeles 4–3 for the franchise's first NBA championship in its 24-year history. Baylor, the Lakers captain, retired early in the 1971–72 season. It was time to let the younger Lakers play and give the team a chance to win it all. The team would go on to win a professional sports record 33 consecutive games, finishing 69–13. In the 1972 finals, they overpowered the Knicks, clinching the Lakers' first NBA championship since 1954.

Looking Back

During his career, Baylor became the standard by which basketball's premier leapers were measured. From 1960 until 1964, he scored at least 20 points in 49 consecutive playoff games. No defense, not even Bill Russell's Celtics, could stop him. In NBA playoff games, Baylor turned his intensity up a notch. In the 1962 playoffs, he scored 30 points or more in 11 straight games. (In comparison, Michael Jordan has an eight-game string of 30-point playoff performances.) Few people remember how strong a rebounder Baylor was. At 6'5", he led the NCAA with 23.5 boards a game in 1958 and averaged 16.4 rebounds (fourth in the NBA) as a rookie and 19.8 boards (fourth again) in 1961. Baylor was as complete a forward as has ever played. He combined the scoring skill of a small forward with the rebounding ability of a power forward. He finished third in the free-throw race in 1961–62, and the following season Baylor finished second in scoring, fifth in assists, fifth in rebounds, and third in free-throw accuracy. The 1963 MVP trophy, however, went to Wilt Chamberlain.

Young players who admired him tried to copy his trademark moves. He changed people's ideas of the game's limits. Though he was dwarfed by giants such as Chamberlain and Russell, he consistently knifed between them or propelled himself over them to score. Players began to emphasize body control in midair, which cannot be taught. Baylor inspired a generation of high-flying players, including Julius Erving, the University of Massachusetts star who was tagged the next Elgin in the early 1970s. Erving went on to have a stellar career in the ABA and NBA. In the 1980s collegians Dominique Wilkins and Michael Jordan were labeled the new Doctor J. Some fans, however, compared Jordan to Baylor.

Baylor played in 7 NBA Finals and 11 All-Star Games. Elgin Baylor retired with 23,149 points; only Michael Jordan and Wilt Chamberlain have higher career scoring averages. Elgin coached the Jazz from 1974 to 1979 (when the franchise played in New Orleans) and currently works as the general manager of the Los Angeles Clippers.

CHAPTER 6

The Big O

Schoolboy basketball is like a religion in Indiana. The state championship tournament is a big deal because every school is entered. The best male player in the state is voted Mr. Basketball. The state is mostly rural and small town, and there are hoops in farmyards, fields, and above barn doors. A 1986 movie about Indiana high school basketball, *Hoosiers*, captures the fervor of basketball fans in Indiana. When a high school wins the state boys basketball tournament, the team parades through their town on fire engines. That tradition is 60 years old.

In the 1950s, Indiana was as racially segregated as Mississippi. The Ku Klux Klan was founded there decades earlier. The majority of state's black residents lived in the cities of Gary and Indianapolis. The best basketball players in Indianapolis came from the Lockfield Gardens housing projects. They played on courts they called the Dust Bowl. In the early 1950s, Lockfield's Bailey "Flap" Robertson set a scoring record at Indianapolis's Crispus Attucks High School. Although Indianapolis public high schools were officially desegregated in the 1940s, Crispus Attucks remained all black. Attucks was coached by math teacher Ray Crowe, whose brother George had played basketball with the Harlem Renaissance and later played major-league baseball. Robertson led Attucks to the state basketball semifinals. No black school had ever gone that far.

People were already talking about Flap's younger brother Oscar, who was holding his own against much older players at the Dust Bowl. In 1955, Gary's Roosevelt High met Crispus Attucks in the first Indiana basketball championship to feature two black schools. Roosevelt starred Richard "Dick" Barnett, who went on to Tennessee State University, where his teams won three straight small college championships, and to the NBA, where he played with the 1970 world champion New York Knicks. Indianapolis officials asked Attucks's principal to guarantee there would be no riots if the team won. A parade route through Indianapolis's black sections was planned for the celebration. Attucks High won the championship, the first black school in Indiana to do so.

Following in his brother's footsteps, Oscar Robertson advanced to Mr. Crowe's Attucks varsity team. He played with a maturity beyond his years. Unlike many products of the school yard, he had no bad habits. He was not flashy like Dick Barnett, who used a stutter-step fake and an exaggerated fall-away jump shot. Fundamentally sound, Oscar threw accurate, lightning passes and handled the ball as if it were on a string. Though he was Attucks's tallest player, he would bring the ball up the court and set up plays. His jump shot was impossible to block because he released it from behind his head with only one palm guiding the ball—textbook perfect. His moves with and without the basketball were fluid. No motion was wasted, and he never did anything simply for show. His quick, strong hands made him an excellent defender, and his understanding of the game helped him think two moves ahead of his opponents. Though he could score at will, Oscar passed unselfishly to teammates in positions for high-percentage shots. He was an excellent foul shooter and a strong rebounder.

Attucks won the 1955 state title with the 6'5" Oscar Robertson playing in the low post and the backcourt and shooting from the wing. His team repeated as state champs a second year. No black school had ever won once before.

Robertson accepted a basketball scholarship at the University of Cincinnati. Situated just north of Kentucky on the Ohio River, Cincinnati had many characteristics of a Southern town, and the Bearcats had never recruited a black player. In 1957, his first varsity season, Oscar was clearly the nation's most complete player. In a game at Madison Square Garden, the sophomore tallied 56 points against Seton Hall, outscoring the Pirates' whole team. No college player has broken his Garden record. That season, he went on to average 35 points a game, more than Seattle's Elgin Baylor and Kansas seven-footer Wilt Chamberlain. Cincinnati compiled a 25–3 record, winning the Missouri Valley Conference. Robertson joined Baylor, Chamberlain, Temple's Guy Rodgers, and Duquesne's Sihugo Green on the All-American first team. It was the first time the team had been composed of five black players.

Cincinnati played in a conference with several southern teams. The other teams, such as Tulsa and Louisville, were all white. In some cities Robertson could not stay with his white teammates in hotels. He would sleep at black-owned hotels or rooming houses. But nothing seemed to frustrate the player nicknamed the Big O. As a junior, Oscar led the NCAA in scoring again, averaging almost 33 points a game as the Bearcats went 26–4. They lost in the national semifinals to the University of California, the eventual champions. Teams assigned two and three players to guard the Big O, but he would either elude them with his arsenal of fakes or score his points at the free-throw line.

The 1960 Bearcats went 28–2. Oscar won the scoring title again, the first player to do so for three seasons running. His 2,973 points shattered the NCAA record, and he held a dozen other college records, including the mark for the most assists in a career. Being the all-time scorer and the all-time setup man for other scorers is a remarkable achievement. What the Big O lacked was a supporting cast of talented teammates to help him win an NCAA championship. His Bearcats were 79–9 over three seasons, and Oscar set 15 school and 13 conference records. The Big O was the territorial draft choice of the NBA's Cincinnati Royals. Black players admired Oscar so much that his college recruited enough schoolboy stars to win back-to-back NCAA titles in 1961 and 1962, the first two years after he left. During the Big O's three-year career, Cincinnati drew 333,548 fans to its home games, compared to 185,244 the previous three years. A cigarette company called its product the Big O, trading on the recognizability of the name.

At the Rome Olympics, Oscar teamed with U.S. stars Walt Bellamy, Jerry Lucas, and Jerry West. International fans marveled at Robertson's ability to alter the tempo of a game. In the gold medal game against the Soviet Union, he led a flurry of fast breaks as the U.S. team went on a 17–1 scoring run that broke open a close game.

After starring on the 1960 Olympic team, which some experts called not only the best Olympic team ever but also the best basketball team ever, Robertson joined the Royals. Never had so much been expected of an NBA rookie—not even of Chamberlain, who had never led the country in scoring and who skipped his senior season to play with the Globetrotters. Oscar was under tremendous pressure. The team had not played well recently, and attendance figures were low. Its first black star, Maurice Stokes, had two great years before an accident on the court confined him to a wheelchair before Robertson was drafted.

Inch for Inch

The Big O did not disappoint Royals fans, many of whom were from racially segregated areas of southern Ohio or Kentucky. Cincinnati drew 25 percent more fans in Robertson's rookie season, and he was named 1961 Rookie of the Year on the strength of his sterling play and imposing stats: 30.5 points, 10.1 rebounds, and 9.7 assists per game. The previous two winners of the award were Elgin Baylor and Wilt Chamberlain. Now the NBA had several black superstars, and white fans were beginning to support them.

In the 1961–62 season, the Big O set a standard that no other NBA player has equaled. He averaged 30.8 points per game and dished out 899 assists for an 11.4 average, which led the league. He also collected 985 rebounds for a 12.5 average—better than any guard before or since. Robertson had averaged double figures in basketball's three key categories: scoring, rebounds, and assists. To have double figures in all three categories in a game is called a triple-double—an exceptional feat that fans began to hear about during the era of Larry Bird and Magic Johnson. A player having a triple-double deserves headlines. Today, such players as Grant Hill, Scottie Pippen, and Jason Kidd are capable of such a game. Oscar Robertson *averaged* triple doubles in 1962, a tribute to his versatility. Coaches and opponents alike were already calling Robertson the greatest player ever to step on a court—and this was the year that Wilt Chamberlain averaged 50 points a game and rang up 100 in a game. Experts considered Oscar the better player inch for inch. The Royals went from 33 wins in 1961 to 43 wins in 1962.

Building the Perfect Player

Imagine a player who could shoot like Glen Rice, pass as well as John Stockton, rebound like Charles Barkley, and defend like Gary Payton and you have some idea of the skill of Oscar Robertson.

Oscar Robertson finished his career with the Milwaukee Bucks. Many experts considered Robertson the best player—inch-for-inch—of his era.

In 1963, 1964, 1965, 1966, and 1967, Oscar Robertson averaged at least 30 points and 10 assists per game. NBA teams in those years averaged about 100 points a night, which meant that Oscar, with his 30 points and the 10 baskets he set up with passes, accounted for half of the Royals' points every night. Guards were seldom asked to rebound much but the Big O led Cincinnati in rebounding twice. His rebounds often led to baskets.

Robertson led the NBA East All-Stars in scoring in six All-Star Games. He was MVP of three All-Star Games, which is a record. In 1964, he was league MVP, the only player other than Russell and Chamberlain to win the award between 1959 and 1968. Fans loved to

Victory in Another Court

On April 16, 1970, Oscar Robertson filed suit against the NBA. In the suit representing all members of the NBA Players Association, Robertson sought to hold up a merger between the NBA and rival ABA until such issues as free agency and freedom of player movement were settled. After six years, the case was settled in the players' favor—two years after Robertson's retirement. The option clause, which bound a player to his original team a year after his contract expired, no longer existed. Robertson had opposed a merger of the NBA and ABA because it would create a monopoly in professional basketball, which would make it impossible for players to negotiate with other teams or jump leagues. The decision in the Robertson suit also enabled players who renounced their college eligibility to apply for the professional draft once their high school class had graduated. It gave the team threatened with losing a player to free agency the right of first refusal to match the contract offered by a new team. When the Robertson suit was settled, 479 NBA players received a total of $4.3 million, and four ABA franchises—New York, Denver, Indiana, and San Antonio—were admitted to the NBA.

watch Russell and Chamberlain's titanic duels, but NBA coaches called Robertson the perfect player. In 1968 he led the league in points and assists, which is like John Stockton or Michael Jordan leading the league in both areas rather than one. He was the league assist leader six times and won two league free-throw titles. When Robertson retired he was the all-time leader in assists (with 9,887 for a 9.5 average) and the second-leading scorer in NBA history, so he has accounted for more baskets than any pro player. Because of his passing and rebounding ability some insist the Big O was a better all-around player than Michael Jordan. He teamed with Lew Alcindor to lead Milwaukee to a four-game sweep over the Baltimore Bullets in the 1971 NBA Finals.

The great Celtics coach Red Auerbach said of Robertson, "Other players hurt you in one way, scoring, rebounding or playmaking, but Oscar hurts you all ways. He's the complete player." Every season between 1960 and 1965, Oscar Robertson and Guy Rodgers finished either first or second in assists in the NBA. Oscar averaged 30 points a game in six of his first eight seasons, and more than 28 the other two. His lifetime playoff rebound average is 6.7.

CHAPTER 7

Maurice and Jack

Maurice Stokes was a star high school basketball player from Pittsburgh who became a college All-American at an unlikely school: St. Francis of Loretto, Pennsylvania. In one college game he snatched 39 rebounds. In 1955, the NBA's Rochester Royals selected Stokes. His numbers with the 1955–56 Royals are a testament to his versatility. The 6'7" 240-pounder averaged 16.8 points, 16.3 rebounds, and 4.9 assists. For a man his size, he was surprisingly quick. Stokes was named Rookie of the Year in 1956. Royals fans were excited about their new star.

The Rochester owner decided that he could no longer afford the Royals and sold the team to a group in Cincinnati. That left the league with the Syracuse Nationals as the only upstate New York team. Cincinnati welcomed the Royals, a young team with budding talents Maurice Stokes and Jack Twyman, a 6'6" jump shooter from the University of Cincinnati. Stokes did not disappoint the fans. His ferocity on the backboards belied his mild-mannered, bespectacled appearance. He averaged 15.6 points, 17.4 rebounds (to lead the NBA), and 4.6 assists in 1956–57. In his third season, 1957–58, Cincinnati won only 33 of 72 games, but Mo Stokes scored almost 17 points a game and averaged 18 rebounds and 6.4 assists per contest—the latter figure excellent for a guard, rare even for a center. Royals fans were licking their chops at the prospect of Stokes and Jack Twyman being joined by their eventual territorial draft choice, University of Cincinnati sophomore Oscar Robertson. Maybe Cincinnati would become an NBA powerhouse.

On March 15, 1958, the Royals were scheduled to begin a playoff round in a televised game against Detroit. Cincinnati players noticed that Stokes, who usually joked about getting ready to play well on television, was abnormally quiet. Teammates dismissed Stokes's low-key mood. The big forward had a boil on his neck, and in the season's last game against the Lakers, he was involved in a collision resulting in a blow to his head. That had been three days earlier.

Maurice played 39 minutes against Detroit. His 12 points and 15 rebounds were substandard for him. After a snack at the hotel, he returned to his room, where he asked a teammate to open the window so he could get some air. The Royals left the hotel for the Detroit airport to return to Cincinnati for game two. "Get a doctor," asked Stokes. "I feel like I'm going to die." No doctor was available, and take-off time was only minutes away. During the flight Stokes vomited, but some players thought perhaps he had had too many beers between the season's end and the playoffs. They left him alone. The Cincinnati owners and NBA commissioner Maurice Podoloff were on the plane.

Stokes became violently ill, with labored breathing. A stewardess gave him oxygen, which may have saved his life. Stokes lapsed into a coma, frightening everyone aboard. The pilot radioed for an ambulance to meet the jet on the runway in Cincinnati. After hospitalization, the man who had been Rookie of the Year just two years earlier was diagnosed with brain damage to the motor control center. Two months earlier, baseball's premier catcher, the Dodgers's Roy Campanella, had been paralyzed in an automobile accident on an icy New York road. Two of America's most popular black athletes had fallen victim to permanent injuries. Stokes was not only immobilized but also could not speak. His family from Pittsburgh came to Cincinnati whenever possible, but job obligations limited their visits. Maurice was confined to Cincinnati's Good Samaritan Hospital.

Though Mo's incapacitation tore all his teammates' hearts, Jack Twyman was particularly moved by Stokes's plight. Whereas other players would leave the city in the off-season, Twyman, a Cincinnati resident, stayed in the city. He felt responsible for his hospitalized former teammate. Twyman realized how expensive Stokes's medical care could be, and doctors had no idea how long he would remain unconscious. Twyman thought of Maurice's family in Pittsburgh and how inconvenient it was for them to visit Cincinnati. Doctors were against moving Maurice to Pittsburgh. Twyman asked the Stokes family if he could become Maurice's legal guardian. It was a big decision. They were a very close-knit family, but Twyman's offer made sense: Jack was a caring individual and a Cincinnati player. Stokes's parents consented to Twyman assuming guardianship of their son.

The story of the tragedy and the friendship between the black and white player made headlines. In 1958, much of the United States was racially segregated. Blacks in southern states could not vote or attend their state universities. The bonding of the two Royals players touched people everywhere. It showed the nation that friendship had no color. In 1959, Kutscher's Country Club in New York's Catskills Mountains, where Wilt Chamberlain had once been a bellboy, offered to sponsor a charity basketball game for Maurice Stokes if the NBA's best players would participate. All the great players immediately responded. Chamberlain flew in from Paris, where he was playing with the Globetrotters, at his own expense. After the benefit game Wilt took a helicopter to New York and then caught a plane back to Paris.

Jack Twyman shows Maurice Stokes the Most Courageous Athletes awards that they received from the Philadelphia Sports Writers Association in 1962. With the civil rights movement in full swing, the close relationship between Twyman and Stokes demonstrated that blacks and whites could be friends.

Through sheer will, Stokes made some progress. The doctor provided him with a specially equipped wheelchair. Stokes had difficulty feeding himself and could only take a few steps by leaning against parallel bars. Twyman's care seemed to encourage him. After the 1960 Kutscher's Maurice Stokes benefit game, Jack told Maurice the details of the game: what the Big O and Wilt did. Twyman continued to play well for Cincinnati, averaging 31 points in 1959–60 and 25.3 as Oscar Robertson's teammate in 1960–61. In his 11-year NBA career, he averaged 19.2 points per game and once played in 609 consecutive games.

By 1967 Jack Twyman had retired from the NBA, became a successful realtor and endorsed various basketball products. In the summer of 1967, Maurice Stokes's physicians agreed to allow the former star to attend the annual Kutscher's charity game in his name. Stokes flew to the Catskills in a private plane. During the events, the onetime fearless rebounder was as cheerful as a small child, and his presence and courage inspired the all-stars on hand. In 1970, Stokes finally succumbed to his injuries, dying at age 37. A few years later, a movie called *Big Mo* was made about his friendship with Jack Twyman. In 1982, Jack Twyman was inducted into the Basketball Hall of Fame.

CHAPTER 8

Shooting Stars

Of the many black stars of the 1960s, Sam Jones and Hal Greer stand out. Both Hall of Famers were deadly accurate shooters and played on teams considered to be among the best in NBA history.

Sam Jones

At Laurinburg Institute, an all-male academy for black high school students in North Carolina, Frank McDuffie was a teacher and basketball coach for years. (Laurinburg was a well-known school; jazz trumpeter Dizzy Gillespie was a graduate.) McDuffie taped a horizontal strip above the basket for his players to aim at because any shot that hit the strip would fall into the hoop. The player who benefited most from this practice was a long-legged North Carolinian named Sam Jones. He was so good that when he graduated from Laurinburg in 1951 he could sink shots from any angle without shooting at the basket from the front. Along with Williston Industrial's Meadowlark Lemon, Jones was the most highly recruited black high school player in North Carolina. (Lemon went to become the Clown Prince of Basketball with the Harlem Globetrotters for 30 years.) Jones grew to 6'4", and his hand-eye coordination made him an excellent tennis, baseball, and basketball player.

Jones planned on playing college basketball at City College of New York (CCNY), which had recently won the NCAA and NIT tournaments. A betting scandal at CCNY, however, changed Sam's mind. Notre Dame showed some interest, but like other schools with good baseball programs, they did not recruit Jones enthusiastically because it was assumed he would also play basketball, a strenuous sport with a long season that ended right before baseball's began. Sam picked North Carolina College (NCC) in Durham, North Carolina. (NCC is now North Carolina Central University.) The black school had just hired Floyd Brown to replace departing coach John McLendon, who had accepted the coaching job at Hampton Institute.

North Carolina College, like most black universities of that period, invited freshman athletes to work the summer prior to their first classes. Sam Jones worked in the morning before lunch. After he ate, he played pickup games in the Eagles gym against players from the basketball team. In those games with "Tree" Taylor, Fox Ramey, and Ernie "Hands" Warlick (who later became a Buffalo Bills wide receiver), Jones held his own. Although coach McDuffie's tape was not there, Sam knew where the spot was, and he could hit it consistently.

Sam was an All-Conference player at NCC, the best shooter and fastest player in a very competitive conference. In a college league that later produced such celebrated players as NBA stars Earl Monroe, Rick Mahorn, and Charles Oakley and Globetrotters "Jumpin" Jackie Jackson and Curly Neal, Sam became the first to play in the NBA. But it was not that easy. Black college sports were covered by the black press only. NCC's games were not televised, and they didn't play against the established programs at segregated schools

119

such as Duke and North Carolina. Players in the Atlantic Coast Conference, however, did know of players in the CIAA, the mid-Atlantic conference of black colleges in which Sam played.

The Minneapolis Lakers heard about Sam from Bob "Slick" Leonard, a tricky white guard who played against Sam in army ball. In 1956, Jones turned down an offer to sign with the Lakers in order to return to college and finish working for his degree. Had Sam gone with the Lakers, NBA history would have been quite different. The Lakers used the pick for flamboyant West Virginia guard Rodney "Hot Rod" Hundley instead.

Before the 1957 NBA draft, Red Auerbach asked Wake Forest basketball coach Bones McKinney whether he knew of any good players. Pro basketball scouting wasn't very sophisticated 40 years ago, and most pro teams did not scout black colleges. McKinney had played for Auerbach on the old Washington Capitols in the BAA, and Auerbach valued his judgment. McKinney knew basketball in the region, and he knew about Sam Jones because he followed CIAA basketball. McKinney told Auerbach, "I saw a boy named Sam Jones in a game at Winston-Salem this winter. He's got a great shot, and he's the fastest man I've ever seen on a basketball court. If I were you I'd grab him." Because of that phone call, Jones became a teammate of Russell's and Havlicek's.

When Bob Cousy first saw Jones running wind sprints at Celtics preseason training he said, "He's the fastest human being I've ever seen on a basketball floor." Red Auerbach took to saying of Sam, "He has wings on his Converse." Jones could not crack the Boston starting lineup as a rookie. Like K. C. Jones, he was a back-up player. The Celtics had the NBA's best veteran backcourt: sharpshooter Bill Sharman and ballhandling genius Bob Cousy. Sam was the third black player to make the Celtic roster.

Auerbach had the NBA's best-conditioned team, which they had to be to play his pressure defense and run their deadly fast break. Sportswriters and broadcasters called K. C. and Sam the Jones Boys.

Both guards knew they could have started elsewhere, but they stayed with Boston, observing Auerbach's bench strategies and Cousy and Sharman's floor play. It didn't make sense to leave a championship team to get more minutes with another team. Cousy and Sharman had been Celtics since 1951, and they would soon be retire.

Bill Sharman led the NBA in free-throw percentage seven times before retiring in 1961. and Bob Cousy led the league in assists eight times in a row before his 1963 retirement. In their own way, the Joneses were just as effective when they took over. K. C. was always assigned the opponents' best scoring guard, whether it was Jerry West, Oscar Robertson, or Hal Greer. His philosophy was to always force the offensive player to make one more dribble, shoot an instant sooner, or go in a different direction than he wanted to. K. C. revolutionized guard play, harassing the other team's ball handler all over the court, challenging every pass, playing chest-to-chest defense.

As soon as Bill Sharman retired, Sam Jones displayed his worth. He averaged 18 to 19 points every year between 1962 and 1964. On the 1964–65 Celtics, considered one of the best teams in NBA history, Sam took 1,818 shots, compared to his previous high of 1,359. The increased shooting resulted in Sam's 25.9 scoring average, an uncharacteristically high figure for a Celtic. Boston played a team style so balanced that no one had ever averaged more than 22.5 points.

Jones favored the bank shot, and no NBA player has ever made such a living off the glass. When Sam was hot, he couldn't miss. He stroked it so well that from 1960 through 1966 he had a better field-goal percentage than the Celtics' center, Bill Russell. For a guard to lead his team in shooting was remarkable. Sam led Boston in scoring for seven years in a row, and in 1965 and 1967 he was their best foul shooter. The only other NBA guard who could run the court with Jones was Hal Greer, who was perhaps the second fastest player of the 1960s.

Sam Jones retired after the 1969 championship, the same year that Bill Russell called it quits. Sam had played in 154 playoff games,

In a 1964 game, Sam Jones tries to beat the Knicks'
Bob Boozer off the dribble. Known for his deadly accurate bank
shots, Jones was a key player in the great Celtics dynasty.

averaging 18.9 points, which was a lot considering he played behind Cousy for six seasons. His career regular-season average was 17.7, though on a different team he could have averaged much more. Even though Sam was the contemporary of such standout guards as Oscar Robertson, Jerry West, Lenny Wilkens, Guy Rodgers, and Hal Greer, he played in nine All-Star games. A year after his retirement, Jones became the first athletic director at Federal City College (now part of the University of the District of Columbia). He was named to the Basketball Hall of Fame in 1983, the second black Celtics player so honored.

Hal Greer

Hal Greer attended Huntington High School in Huntington, West Virginia, then became the first black athlete at Marshall University in West Virginia. Greer was a college senior in 1958, the same year Elgin Baylor and Guy Rodgers were seniors. It was not a deep draft crop, but Greer was one of the country's best guards. He had ushered in the era of the 100-point game at Marshall.

Greer's college coach was Jules Rivlin; Paul Seymour, coach of the Syracuse Nationals, was one of Rivlin's former players. Rivlin sold Seymour on Hal Greer. A charter member of the NBA, the Nats were always a playoff team but never a power in the East. Greer joined a team that had been led by the same scoring leader, 6'8" forward Dolph Schayes, from 1950 to 1961. (Schayes's son Danny played in the NBA.) The Nats' other steady players were guard Larry Costello and center Johnny "Big Red" Kerr.

The Nats' veterans reached out to Greer, but he was not an immediate sensation. He started his career as a role player, but when Dolph Schayes got older, Greer took up the offensive slack. In 1961–62, Hal averaged 22.8 points a game. He led the Nats in scoring (19.5) and minutes played the following season, the franchise's last season in

Hall-of-Famer Hal Greer was a slick ballhander, tenacious defender, and feared shooter.

Syracuse. In 1963, Irv Kasloff and Ike Richman bought the Nats and moved them to Philadelphia, and the team was renamed the 76ers.

In the 1963–64 season Hal Greer emerged as the Sixers' marquee player. He led them in scoring (23.3), free-throw percentage (82.9), and assists (4.7). The 76ers, coached by Dolph Schayes, won only 34 of 78 games, 14 fewer than the previous season. In 1964, the 76ers welcomed a new player, Wilt Chamberlain. This hometown product had played in Philly for the Warriors before they moved to the Bay area. With Wilt setting picks for Greer, Hal got more open shots. More important, he had the ultimate teammate to share the scoring burden with. Hal led the 1964–65 Sixers in assists, but the team won only half their games. They were beaten by Boston in the Eastern finals, in the famous seventh game in which Greer's inbounds pass was stolen by John Havlicek. It was more a great defensive play by Havlicek than an error by Greer.

The 1965–66 Sixers had an influx of young talent: forward Chet Walker, a 6'7" former All-American at Bradley; Billy Cunningham, a slashing left-hander who had starred at North Carolina; hometown favorite Wally Jones, a streak shooter out of Villanova; and strongman Lucius Jackson, a 6'9", 240-pounder from Pan American, the prototype for today's power forwards. This squad appeared ready to challenge the veteran Celtics.

Philly won the NBA East in 1966, with a 55–25 mark. They got their first playoff bye, granting them a week of rest while Boston dueled with Cincinnati. The time off hurt their game, and Boston wiped out Philly 4–1 in the Eastern finals. Alex Hannum replaced Dolph Schayes as coach for the 1966–67 season. Hannum convinced Chamberlain to shoot less. Wilt had never played with as many good scorers—Jones, Cunningham, Walker, and Greer—and the unit quickly jelled. Greer and Jones gunned from the perimeter, and Walker and Cunningham knifed in for layups. On defense, Wilt and Jackson discouraged drives to the hoop. The team won 45 of its first 49 games. Their final record was 68–13, the league's best ever at that time. The unselfish Chamberlain rediscovered the hot passing that he had learned as a Globetrotter, palming the ball high above his head at arm's length as teammates cut toward the hoop. Chamberlain averaged 7.8 assists for the season. The 76ers cruised past the Celtics 4–1 in the Eastern playoffs and then beat San Francisco 4–2 in the NBA championship. Hal Greer, the playoff goat of 1965, was saved from eternal disgrace.

Sports fans wondered whether the 76ers were merely a fluke. Had Boston just taken a year's leave of their reign? Philly's one championship, no matter how impressive their won-loss mark, paled in comparison to Boston's nine straight banners. The Sixers moved into a new home for the 1967–68 season, the 15,000 seat Spectrum. The 1968 NBA All-Star Game was a showcase for Hal Greer. In the third quarter, Greer shot 8 for 8. He finished with 19 points and was voted Most Valuable Player. Greer also had his best season that year, averaging 24.1 points. When defenders double-teamed Wilt, Greer sprinted to the top of the key and fired his deadly jump shot. From 15 to 18 feet out, he was as dangerous a shooter as Oscar Robertson. At 6'3", 185 pounds, he was an athletic defender.

From 1961 to 1967, Jerry West and Oscar Robertson were the All-NBA first team guards, while Hal Greer and Sam Jones were second team. Many rated Greer right behind West and Robertson, the league's elite guards. Hal Greer scored 21,586 points in his career and had a 20.4-point career average in 92 playoff games, including a 25.8 clip in the 1968 playoffs. Greer retired with an NBA record for minutes played, almost 40,000. He was one of few men to play in three decades and averaged 20 points in eight seasons. In 1981 he was named to the Basketball Hall of Fame.

CHAPTER 9

Past and Present

Fifty years ago, baseball was far and away the most popular sport with American youth. It had the most media coverage, was easy to play with friends, and the best major-league players were household names. In 1947, a black player, Jackie Robinson, integrated major-league baseball. Robinson's early success made playing big-league baseball a realistic goal for black children and drew many new black fans to the game. Three years after Robinson's breakthrough, Chuck Cooper, Earl Lloyd, and Nat Clifton integrated the NBA. Because professional basketball was still in its infancy, this development was greeted by far less national fanfare than Jackie Robinson's debut. Yet Cooper, Lloyd, and Clifton endured the same racial slurs and indignities from fans and opponents that Robinson experienced. (Even later superstars, such as Bill Russell and Oscar Robertson, endured NBA road-trips that included segregated hotels and restaurants.)

The Greatest Ever?

How do we measure the greatest players ever? Is consistency the hallmark? Or longevity? Championships or astronomical statistics? Or a combination of these factors? Who was the greatest?

Supporters of Earvin "Magic" Johnson point to his multifaceted game, his winning ways, and his assist titles. He made those who played with him better and added years to Kareem Abdul-Jabbar's career. Those who insist Bill Russell was the greatest of all time argue that his 11 championships in 13 seasons, his intimidating defense, his rebounding, and his cerebral approach render all dissenting debate pointless. Chamberlain fanatics stress Wilt's superhuman strength, otherworldly stats, and his play on the second- and third-winningest teams in NBA history. Delegates for Oscar Robertson mention his scoring skills, his perennial assist leadership, and his 1962 season achievement of averaging a triple-double. The Michael Jordan camp base their case on Jordan's championship rings, his combination of scoring and defense, his unstoppable one-on-one moves, his performance in clutch situations, and his leadership on the winningest team in NBA history.

The dignity with which these early black NBA players rose above racial obstacles paved the way for today's NBA superstars. The popularity of the televised "duals" between Russell and Wilt Chamberlain in the intense Boston-Philadelphia games transformed the NBA into a major sports league, and Elgin Baylor's aerial artistry set the stage for a succession of high-flying stars, including Julius Erving and Michael Jordan.

When they stepped on the court in 1950, Cooper, Lloyd, and Clifton were representing an entire race. Unlike today's players—too many of whom are suspended or fined for fighting, missing practices, or abusing drugs—the NBA's first players had no margin of error. Any unwise behavior, on or off the court, would have served as an excuse to bar black players forever. The black pioneers of professional basketball understood this pressure, and their positive reaction to it opened the game up for the players who have made the NBA the overwhelming success it is today with youth all over the world.

A Note on Sources

I used many books and sources in writing *Sky Kings*. For a general history of the NBA, I consulted *From Cagers to Jump Shots* (New York: Oxford University Press, 1994) by Robert W. Peterson and *24 Seconds to Shoot* (New York: Macmillan, 1968) by Leonard Koppett. These books chronicled the NBA's integration in 1950. For information on Bill Russell, his autobiography as told to Taylor Branch, *Second Wind* (New York: Random House, 1979), and Neil D. Isaacs's *All the Moves* were valuable sources. The primary information on Wilt Chamberlain was researched in his autobiography with David Shaw, *Wilt* (New York: Macmillan, 1973).

The Black Athlete, a volume in the International Library of Afro-American Life & History (Publishers Agency, 1976), was my main guide on the careers of Oscar Robertson, Hal Greer, Elgin Baylor, Sam Jones, and K. C. Jones. Terry Pluto's *Tall Tales* (New York:

Simon & Schuster, 1992) is an oral history of the NBA; former players, coaches, and referees reflect on the league from its conception through the 1960s. *Tall Tales* helped me trace the NBA's growth from regional novelty to major league status and provided assessments of Oscar Robertson, Wilt Chamberlain, and Elgin Baylor by their contemporaries.

NBA statistics within the general text were gathered from the annual The *Official NBA Basketball Encyclopedia* (New York: New American Library, annual), edited by Zander Hollander and Alex Sachare. The college statistics of Baylor, Russell, Chamberlain, and Robertson were collected from four sources: Isaacs's *All the Moves*, Chamberlain and Shaw's *Wilt*, Arthur Ashe's *A Hard Road to Glory* (New York: Amistad, 1988), and *The Black Athlete*.

For information on various specific topics, please consult the reading list on the following page.

For Further Reading

Ashe, Arthur, Jr., ed. *A Hard Road To Glory*. New York: Amistad, 1994.

Berkow, Ira. *Oscar Robertson: The Golden Year*. New York: Prentice Hall, 1992.

Dickey, Glenn. *The History of Professional Basketball*. New York: University Press of America, 1982.

Frankl, Ron. *Wilt Chamberlain*. New York: Chelsea House, 1994.

Libby, Bill. *Goliath: The Wilt Chamberlain Story*. New York: Dodd, Mead, 1968.

Nadel, Eric. *The Night Wilt Scored One Hundred: Tales from Basketball's Past*. Taylor, 1990.

Peterson, Robert W. *From Cages to Jumpshots*. New York: Oxford University Press, 1968.

Pluto, Terry. *Loose Balls: The Short, Wild Life of the American Basketball Association*. New York: Simon & Schuster, 1991.

———. *Tall Tales*. New York: Simon & Schuster, 1992.

Russell, Bill, as told to William McSweeny. *Go Up For Glory*. New York: Berkeley-Coward, 1966.

Shapiro, Miles. *Bill Russell*. New York: Chelsea House, 1991.

Wohl, David. *Foul! The Connie Hawkins Story*. New York: Fireside, 1988.

Appendix

Career Statistics for Selected Sky Kings

Elgin Baylor

season, team	*games played*	*assists/game*	*rebounds/game*	*points/game*
Minneapolis				
1958–59	70	4.1	15.0	24.9
1959–60	70	3.5	16.4	29.6
Los Angeles				
1960–61	73	5.1	19.8	34.8
1961–62	48	4.6	18.6	38.3
1962–63	80	4.8	14.3	34.0
1963–64	78	4.4	12.0	25.4
1964–65	74	3.8	12.8	27.1
1965–66	65	3.4	9.6	16.6
1966–67	70	3.1	12.8	26.6
1967–68	77	4.6	12.2	26.0
1968–69	76	5.4	10.6	24.8
1969–70	54	5.4	10.4	24.0

1970–71	2	1.0	5.5	10.0
1971–72	9	2.0	6.3	11.8
Career Totals	*846*	*4.3*	*13.5*	*27.4*
Playoff Totals	*134*	*4.0*	*12.9*	*27.0*

Career Highlights: All-Star Game MVP (1959); NBA Rookie of the Year (1959); scored 71 points in one game (1960); played in 11 All-Star Games; known for his ability to score in the air; retired as third-leading all-time NBA scorer; inducted into Basketball Hall of Fame in 1976; selected to the NBA's 50th Anniversary All-Time Players List in 1996

Wilt Chamberlain

season, team	games played	assists/game	rebounds/game	points/game
Philadelphia				
1959–60	72	2.3	27.0	37.6
1960–61	79	1.9	27.2	38.4
1961–62	80	2.4	25.7	50.4
San Francisco				
1962–63	80	3.4	24.3	44.8
1963–64	80	5.0	22.3	36.9
S.F., Philadelphia				
1964–65	73	3.4	22.9	34.7
Philadelphia				
1965–66	79	5.2	24.6	33.5
1966–67	81	7.8	4.2	24.1
1967–68	82	8.6	23.8	24.3
Los Angeles				
1968–69	81	4.5	21.1	20.5
1969–70	12	4.1	18.4	27.3
1970–71	82	4.3	18.2	20.7
1971–72	82	4.0	19.2	14.8

1972–73	82	4.5	18.6	13.2
Career Totals	*1045*	*4.4*	*22.9*	*30.1*
Playoff Totals	*160*	*4.2*	*24.5*	*22.5*

Career Highlights: Holds NBA record for points in a season (4,029), points in a game (100), scoring average for a season (50.4), rebounds in a game (55), rebounds in a season (2,149), career rebounds (23,924); led NBA in assists (1967–68); NBA MVP four times; played in 13 All-Star Games; inducted into Basketball Hall of Fame in 1978; selected to the NBA's 50th Anniversary All-Time Players List in 1996

Hal Greer

season, team	games played	assists/game	rebounds/game	points/game
Syracuse				
1958–59	68	1.5	2.9	11.1
1959–60	70	2.7	4.3	13.2
1960–61	79	3.8	5.8	19.6
1961–62	71	4.4	7.4	22.8
1962–63	80	3.4	5.7	19.5
Philadelphia				
1963–64	80	4.7	6.1	23.3
1964–65	70	4.5	5.1	20.2
1965–66	80	4.8	5.9	22.7
1966–67	80	3.8	5.3	22.1
1967–68	82	4.5	5.4	24.1
1968–69	82	5.0	5.3	23.1
1969–70	80	5.1	4.7	22.0
1970–71	81	4.6	4.5	18.6
1971–72	81	3.9	3.3	11.8
1972–73	38	2.9	2.8	5.6
Career Totals	*1122*	*4.0*	*5.0*	*19.2*
Playoff Totals	*92*	*4.3*	*5.5*	*20.4*

Career Highlights: Spent entire 15-year career with the same team; known for his sharpshooting; played in 10 All-Star Games; inducted into Basketball Hall of Fame in 1981; selected to the NBA's 50th Anniversary All-Time Players List in 1996

K. C. Jones

season, team	games played	assists/game	rebounds/game	points/game
Boston				
1958–59	49	1.4	2.6	3.5
1959–60	74	2.6	2.7	6.3
1960–61	78	3.2	3.6	7.6
1961–62	80	4.3	3.7	9.2
1962–63	79	4.0	3.3	7.2
1963–64	80	5.1	4.7	8.2
1964–65	78	5.6	4.1	8.3
1965–66	80	6.3	3.8	8.6
1966–67	78	5.0	3.1	6.2
Career Totals	*676*	*4.3*	*3.5*	*7.4*
Playoff Totals	*105*	*3.8*	*3.0*	*6.4*

Career Highlights: played on eight Celtics championship teams in his nine-year career; defensive specialist; coached Celtics teams that won two NBA titles (1984, 1986); inducted into Basketball Hall of Fame in 1988

Sam Jones

season, team	games played	assists/game	rebounds/game	points/game
Boston				
1957–58	56	0.7	2.9	4.6
1958–59	71	1.4	6.0	10.7
1959–60	74	1.7	5.1	11.9

1960–61	78	2.8	5.4	15.0
1961–62	78	3.0	5.9	18.4
1962–63	76	3.2	5.2	19.7
1963–64	76	2.7	4.6	19.4
1964–65	80	2.8	5.1	25.9
1965–66	67	3.2	5.2	23.5
1966–67	72	3.0	4.7	22.1
1967–68	73	3.0	4.9	21.3
1968–69	70	2.6	3.8	16.3
Career Totals	*871*	*2.5*	*4.9*	*17.7*
Playoff Totals	*154*	*2.3*	*4.7*	*18.9*

Career Highlights: Played on ten Celtics championship teams; known for his sweet bank shots; inducted into Basketball Hall of Fame in 1983; selected to the NBA's 50th Anniversary All-Time Players List in 1996

Oscar Robertson

season, team	games played	assists/game	rebounds/game	points/game
Cincinnati				
1960–61	71	9.7	10.1	30.5
1961–62	79	11.4	12.5	30.8
1962–63	80	9.5	10.4	28.3
1963–64	79	11.0	9.9	31.4
1964–65	75	11.5	9.0	30.4
1965–66	76	11.1	7.7	31.3
1966–67	79	10.7	6.2	30.5
1967–68	65	9.7	6.0	29.2
1968–69	79	9.8	6.4	24.7
1969–70	69	8.1	6.1	25.3
Milwaukee				
1970–71	81	8.2	5.7	19.4
1971–72	64	7.7	5.0	17.4

1972–73	73	7.5	4.9	15.5
1973–74	70	6.4	4.0	12.7
Career Totals	**1040**	**9.5**	**7.5**	**25.7**
Playoff Totals	**86**	**8.9**	**6.7**	**22.2**

Career Highlights: NBA Rookie of the Year (1961); averaged a triple-double in 1961–62; league MVP (1964); three-time All-Star Game MVP (1961, 1964, 1969); known for his all-around game; inducted into Basketball Hall of Fame in 1979; selected to the NBA's 50th Anniversary All-Time Players List in 1996

Bill Russell

season, team	games played	assists/game	rebounds/game	points/game
Boston				
1956–57	48	1.8	19.6	14.7
1957–58	69	2.9	2.7	16.6
1958–59	70	3.2	23.0	16.7
1959–60	74	3.7	24.0	18.2
1960–61	78	3.4	23.9	16.9
1961–62	76	4.5	23.6	18.9
1962–63	78	4.5	23.6	16.8
1963–64	78	4.7	24.7	15.0
1964–65	78	5.3	24.1	14.1
1965–66	78	4.8	22.8	12.9
1966–67	81	5.8	21.0	3.3
1967–68	78	4.6	18.6	12.5
1968–69	77	4.9	19.3	9.9
Career Totals	**963**	**4.3**	**22.5**	**15.1**
Playoff Totals	**165**	**4.7**	**24.9**	**16.2**

Career Highlights: played on 11 Celtics championship teams; appeared in 12 All-Star Games; All-Star Game MVP (1963); five-time NBA MVP (years); won two championships as Celtics player-coach

(1968, 1969); defensive prowess changed the game; inducted into Basketball Hall of Fame in 1974; selected to the NBA's 50th Anniversary All-Time Players List in 1996

Maurice Stokes

season, team	games played	assists/game	rebounds/game	points/game
Rochester				
1955–56	67	4.9	16.3	16.8
1956–57	72	4.6	17.4	15.6
Cincinnati				
1957–58	63	6.4	18.1	16.9
Career Totals	*202*	*5.3*	*17.3*	*16.4*
Playoff Totals	*1*	*2.0*	*15.0*	*12.0*

Career Highlights: NBA Rookie of the Year (1956); promising career ended by head injury that resulted in brain damage (1958); relationship with teammate Jack Twyman showed nation that blacks and whites could be friends

Index

Page numbers in *italics* indicate illustrations.